AT HOME WITH JAPANESE DESIGN

JEAN MAHONEY
PEGGY LANDERS RAO

PHOTOGRAPHS BY
TOSHIAKI SAKUMA

AT HOME WITH JAPANESE DESIGN

ACCENTS, STRUCTURE AND SPIRIT

SHUFUNOTOMO CO., LTD.
TOKYO

For Don,
surefooted with a gypsy in his soul,
and for Jeanette and Ellen
who have always enjoyed the ride.

© Copyright 1990 in Japan.
by Peggy Landers Rao and Jean Mahoney

First printing, 1990
Second printing, 1991

Published by Shufunotomo Co., Ltd.
2-9, Kanda Surugadai Chiyoda-ku, Tokyo, 101 Japan

Printed in Japan

ISBN 4-07-975061-7

Art Direction and Book Design
by Jean Mahoney

TABLE OF CONTENTS

*For Jagadish
who has always known that sometimes
you have to go East to get West,
and for Maya, Amar and Abby
who make the best of both worlds.*

Additional photo credits:
Page 49 (above) — Katsuhiko Ushiro from the book,
                  Table Talk, published by Bunka
                  Publishing Bureau.
Page 93 — Bill Rothschild
Page 107 (right) — Koichi Taniguchi
         (left) — Shufunotomo
Pages 46, 47, 59-61, 63-65, 70, 138 — Jean Mahoney
Pages 46, 62, 69 — Peggy Rao

NOTE: In the Japanese language, nouns do not change
their form to indicate plurals. Therefore, when using a
Japanese word in this book, we have retained its unvarying
form in both singular and plural contexts.

We are grateful to many people whose help made this project possible and whose enthusiasm made it such a pleasure.

Special thanks are due those who introduced us to various locations or allowed us to pepper them with questions: Barbara Kehoe, Mary Olive, Wren Okasaki, Jeff Cline, Kim Nelson and Tim Mertel on the West Coast. Maryell Semal and Leighton Longhi in New York; Sadato Kurotake and Yoshinori Osugi in Kyoto; John Adair, Yuko Arai, Naomi Kojima, Masaru Saito and Yoshihiro Saito in Tokyo.

We were fortunate, too, in receiving valuable suggestions regarding the manuscript from Alice North, Blanche Healey and Elizabeth Mulvihill, who remained unflappable under the pressure of deadlines. And again, we salute our editor, Shun-ichi Kamiya, whose range of talents never ceases to amaze us; and our photographer, Toshiaki Sakuma, whose artistic eye and technical mastery so beautifully captured our discoveries. We are privileged to have them as partners and friends.

Finally and most importantly, we would like to thank the many talented people who graciously opened their doors to us and to our readers.

Japan

John A. Adair, Jr.
David Baran
Lisbeth and Carter Beise
Major General and Mrs. Matthew Cooper
Lieutenant General and Mrs. J.B. Davis
Colette and René Flipo
Naomi Iwasaki Hoff
Renée and Dan Kubiak
Cindi Novkov
Marilyn and Chikafusa Sato
Puang and Fritz Schmitz
Per Schmølcher
Ann and Chris Seddon
Reiko and Yoshihiro Takishita
Kenji Tsuchisawa
Anne Ward, Isetan Department Store
Kate and Don Wiest
Martine and Rudi Zingg

California

Dr. and Mrs. Robert Beeman
Barbara and Robert Kehoe
Dr. and Mrs. Hayman Gong
Emily Newell
James Porter
Alma and Leo Shapiro
Kathleen and Michael Sparer
Lequita Vance-Watkins

Connecticut

June Laben

Hawaii

Amaury Saint-Gilles

New York

Erika and Peter A. Aron
Eugénie Au Kim
Mary Griggs Burke
Gioia and Mitchell Brock
Helen Tison Caskey
George Friedman
Susan and Steven Geffen
Eli Horen
Rosemarie and Leighton Longhi
Doris and David Luening
Victoria and Eric V. Lustbader
Sue and Guy Magnuson
Mary McFadden
Alice and Halsey North
John Rogers
Romig and Tal Streeter
Sam Takeuchi
Joanne and Doug Wise
John B. Wisner

New Jersey

Nobuko and Kazumi Shimazaki

Washington

Jeff Cline
Laurie and John Fairman
Kim and George Suyama
Bill Knospe
Paula Devon Raso

Introduction

During our years in Tokyo, we were struck by the ease with which Japanese aesthetics could be blended with a wide range of interior designs. The results of mixing East with West added strength, timelessness and often a quietude to many different kinds of homes. We noticed too, that certain Japanese objects seem to be universally appealing and surprisingly flexible as they appeared in a variety of new situations. Our first book on the subject, *Japanese Accents in Western Interiors,* showed some of the creative ideas found in the homes of various foreign residents in Tokyo who discovered new uses for many Japanese objects.

The welcome accorded that book introduced us to another group of people quite different from the first set of homeowners. Their backgrounds are as diverse as their occupations, but all have roots in Japan one way or another and all have a longtime commitment to Japanese design. They are artists, writers, illustrators, architects, international antique dealers, collectors, interior designers and fashion designers. Their homes mix cultures in ways that are innovative, inspiring and timely. We present the ideas of these 49 wonderful specialists in *At Home with Japanese Design.*

The photos of their homes were taken during a ten-month period. Our team of four — authors, photographer and editor/translator — travelled around Japan and along both coasts of the U.S. taking particular delight again in the people behind the ideas encountered. We met a Japanese antique dealer who has moved farmhouses to places as far away as Switzerland and Argentina. We became acquainted with a French interior designer whose interest in Japanese design was born in Brazil; a Thai university professor whose California tract house is imbued with a Japanese soul; and an American novelist whose settings are medieval Japan, but who has never been to Japan for fear of destroying the images in his mind. We

picnicked in the mountains while on location with a Danish art director working for one of Japan's leading department stores. All seemed to share an appreciation for the serendipitous discoveries of life and all were enthusiastic about sharing their personal expertise with us.

We were also intrigued by how a slight encounter sometimes triggered a lifelong fascination on the part of our subjects. Mary Griggs Burke, who is a recipient of the Japanese government's Honor of the Sacred Treasure, Gold and Silver Star, for collecting and preserving so much of the country's fine art, explained how as a small girl in Minnesota, she fell in love with a striking white-on-black kimono that her mother brought back from Japan just after the turn of the century. "I remember putting it on and letting it trail behind me; I believe a future collector of Japanese art was born then." Eric V. Lustbader, the novelist, recounted how as a teenager he came across Hiroshige's woodblock print "Crossing Nihonbashi" and "that was it." June Laben, a Connecticut dealer in Japanese antiques and the daughter of a collector, recalls making her first acquisition with her own money at the age of seven — an Imari bowl.

As Japan races forward, technologically and economically, we tend to forget its older image of picturesque teahouses and thatched roofs. Yet the design principles and philosophical concepts behind traditional creations have not changed. First-time visitors to Tokyo are surprised to find such a Western-looking city. "Show us the real Japan," they say. The real Japan is still right there behind the chaotic kaleidoscope if they know how to look. Asymmetry, understatement, simplicity, surroundings that are humble by choice are everywhere... in a lacquered dish, the weave of a kimono, the corner of a chest. The unfinished statement is preferable to a complete explanation, which is considered impolite. Everything is tied together, part of the whole fabric of Japanese life where aesthetics and philosophy merge. As the scholar Louis Frédéric put it, "In Japan, the past is always present and the people have remained exactly the same since the beginning of history."

When considering many of the items in this book, it is important to remember the artistic role of many everyday things used by the Japanese. Mary Griggs Burke explains, "The distinction between high art and craft was not so sharply drawn as in the West. Art seemed an indivisible whole, embracing lacquer, ceramics, paintings, textiles, and much more. This aesthetic sensitivity showed in what the people wore, in the utensils they used for eating, and even in the arrangement of food on a plate, as well as in their architecture and masterpieces of sculpture and painting… Japanese art deserves — in fact needs — to be shown in sympathetic ambience in order to reveal all the nuances of its beauty."

At Home with Japanese Design hopes to convey some of those nuances. The camera has focused on harmonious East/West blends while the text attempts to color in the item's long tradition in order to foster greater appreciation. Since caption space does not always allow as much technical description as we would like, we have added a glossary at the end for your reference. We have also indicated the regional sources of many items in Japan when possible, so the reader will be aware of various shopping opportunities outside the usual tourist route. At the end of the book is detailed information on traditional craft centers in various prefectures. This reference material has been supplied by the Japan Traditional Craft Center, a government-supported institution that recognizes 700 locations where traditional crafts have been preserved using the same techniques and materials for at least 100 years.

If there is one constant in this book, apart from the rich artistic experience of the homeowners, it is the resourcefulness exemplified, which is one of Japan's enduring strengths. Lacking rich natural resources, its people have fashioned remarkable objects out of bamboo, clay, paper, straw and other indigenous materials. Village weavers, for example, although limited to primitive backstrap looms which could not provide rich patterns, found other ways to create elaborate designs. Portions of yarns were dyed before weaving to create *kasuri* patterns. Other designs were drawn freehand with a rice paste that resisted dye for the *tsutsugaki* patterns that ornament so many colorful ceremonial pieces. Quilted work coats were given lavish patterns with miniscule stitches. Today, these handcrafted treasures have become collectors' items.

The late Yukiko Maki, acclaimed for her work in cross-cultural understanding, told us on her last visit to the U.S. how she, having been educated in the U.S., learned to become Japanese in the 1920's in the home of her mother-in-law in Tokyo. She was taught to take apart worn cotton kimonos, invert the fabric for new strength and restitch it with new thread. The old thread was saved too, and used for non-critical stitching, not seams. Eventually, after years of washing, an old kimono was cut up, because then it was soft enough to become diapers for a baby's delicate skin. It is this economy of material, this ability to capitalize on what is at hand that Mrs. Maki felt was ingrained in every Japanese, and she believed, contributes to their strength in the business world.

More people are recognizing that Japanese artifacts are too lovely to be left behind in the rush towards the 21st century. This book therefore shows the resourcefulness possible in using various objects or implementing Japanese concepts to make new aesthetic contributions. In *At Home with Japanese Design,* you will find that this resourcefulness knows neither national borders nor interior design limitations.

Tansu: The versatile chest

For the West, it was an immediate romance. No need to know family history. Visitors arriving in Japan in the second half of the 19th century fell in love with Japanese chests, bought them in all sizes and sailed off to put them in prominent spots in their homes.

This surprised the Japanese who never considered their chests as furniture. Since then, more and more of these unpretentious creations have found their way around the world, and are now prized by collectors, favored by designers and welcomed by homeowners, both for their beauty and versatility.

Tansu were never intended to be stationary furniture. They were movable storage boxes kept out of sight in the family's wall cupboard or outside in their storehouse. Yet their careful craftsmanship, which sometimes included false hinges, secret compartments and trick latches, makes them continually appealing.

The best *tansu* are of fairly recent vintage. First appearing in the late 17th century, they reached their zenith at the end of the 19th with several areas producing chests with distinctive regional features.

Each style chest had a specific purpose, particularly during the Edo period (1603-1868) when samurai commissioned *tansu* to reflect their lofty status. Some stored only books or sword blades or tea ceremony utensils. Others yielded medicinal herbs or account books. Many were for specific kinds of clothing. A samurai kept his ceremonial clothing in an *isho-dansu* whose deep drawers could accommodate the "winged" shoulders of his robes. A bride sent her possessions ahead to her husband's family home in her own special chest. Merchants and sea captains adapted chests for their records, and as the chests became more visible, they grew more ornate to impress the customer.

Most chests were readily portable, either carried on shoulder poles inserted through the side handles or rolled on built-in wheels. These huge *kuruma-dansu* (wheeled chests) evolved from a box with a hinged lid, mounted on wheels, in which wealthy families kept most of their possessions. In the event of a fire, it was easy to roll such a trunk out of danger. However, in 1657 a major fire destroyed most of Tokyo and killed 107,000 people, many of whom were trapped in the narrow streets clogged by the enormous chests. Consequently, the government of the Tokugawa Shogun banned the lidded wheeled chest in Tokyo, Kyoto and Osaka, the three most populated cities, and few examples have survived. The wheeled chest with sliding doors and drawers is a later design and is more

Seeming to float above San Francisco, this airy Nob Hill apartment of Alma and Leo Shapiro is counterweighted by the simple strength of a paulownia and cedar clothing chest. Its detailing indicates it originated in Kurume, Kyushu, between 1870-1900 and is one of a pair.

The bowl is by California artist Bill Ellis.

▼ Many small Japanese chests, without legs of their own, pose height problems when combined with Western furniture. Joanne and Doug Wise converted a Meiji era sword chest *(katana-dansu)* into a sofa table for their suburban New York home by having a stand built for it. Mrs. Wise represents contemporary painters, potters and sculptors primarily from Japan. The display on the back shelves includes Bizen ware and Shino ceramics. The teapot and saké cups on the sword chest are by Americans working in the ceramic traditions of Japan, Rob Barnard and Jeff Shapiro.

common today.

One hundred years later, the government again intervened as people vied to own larger and more ornate chests. The sumptuary laws of 1789 which strictly curtailed the merchant and farming classes by regulating their clothing, architecture and even the size of their children's dolls, limited the size and style of chests across the country.

All *tansu* display the Japanese respect for the nature of wood. Veneers were avoided and, unlike European cabinetry, very few rigid joints were used. Seemingly "seamless" surfaces were actually

outstanding examples of joinery that compensated for variations in humidity and the stress of earthquakes.

The most beautiful wood used was zelkova *(keyaki)* which has a flamelike grain and a glowing orange-brown color. Always expensive, it was usually limited to drawer faces and front panels. Cryptomeria or Japanese cedar *(sugi)* and paulownia *(kiri)* were used for the body and drawers. Cryptomeria's smell repels moths and lightweight paulownia can expand and contract indefinitely with changes in humidity without cracking. The interiors were usually

▼ A small chest of the Meiji era (1868-1912), probably for medicinal herbs *(kasuri-dansu)* is raised to a convenient height with a wrought-iron base from Robert Brian Antiques. The San Francisco shop makes supports for many of their small chests. The sink cabinet in this California powder room was designed by Bay Contract Interiors to echo the styling of the antique chests.

▶ Asians often freshen the interior of a chest by papering it. New York designer Susan Paul Geffen took the idea one step further and, instead of refinishing the damaged exterior of her *chō-dansu* (accounts chest), papered the inset panels with pages from an old ledger book.

▼ The richly grained, small zelkova staircase chest *(kaidan-dansu)* is an enduring reminder of the Geffens' years in Japan.

▶ *Opposite page:* A large wheeled chest *(kuruma-dansu)* conceals an array of electronics — TV, stereo, video equipment, discs, tapes — behind its traditional doors. The primitive wooden bowl is made from the river red gum tree of South Australia. As for the lantern, Martine and Rudi Zingg were surprised when it dropped in a Tokyo earthquake, but decided they preferred it that way. The contemporary watercolor is by Kyoto/New York artist Daniel Kelly.

14

left bare, but a transparent lacquer intensified the grain of the zelkova facade.

If a clothing chest was at all visible in the house, its sides generally didn't show, since it was built into the wall. The large clothing chests from the Sendai region in the northeast — some more than seven feet long — were made to fit under the *oshiire,* a built-in closet. While other clothing chests of the era were completely concealed, Sendai chests were placed in prominent positions next to either the family altar or the *tokonoma,* the alcove used to display a scroll and a seasonal flower arrangement. The best Sendai chests date from 1889 to 1900 and are characterized by elaborate hardware in auspicious motifs and zelkova wood stained a deep red. By then, the sumptuary laws had been eliminated and the cabinet makers of Sendai, a mercantile center, began to cater to luxurious tastes.

Experts seem to agree that sea chests *(funa-dansu)* exquisitely crafted in Sakata, a coastal city in Yamagata Prefecture, and Sado Island during the Edo and Meiji periods represent the best

combination of joinery and hardware in the field. In those days, much of internal trade was carried by sea, especially the Inland Sea and the Sea of Japan. The rough handling that these chests received demanded the finest materials and craftsmanship. Zelkova was generally used throughout for strength, and heavy iron hardware was extended to cover much of the front for protection and durability. The chests were of three types: writing boxes, clothing chests, and safes/account boxes to hold the ship's money and documents.

The kitchen *tansu* (*mizuya,* literally "water place") functioned like built-in cabinets, sometimes óccupying a whole wall in the cooking area and holding all utensils and supplies, including jugs of water. Most *mizuya* were made in Shiga Prefecture in the towns between Nagoya and Kyoto. They were often produced without finish, but over the years, developed a patina from the charcoal smoke of the cooking hearth. Even lacquered chests that stood near the fire developed this glow that is prized today.

Staircase chests (*kaidan-dansu*) are perhaps the most memorable of

▶ Country chests take on new elegance in the Park Avenue living room of Erika and Peter A. Aron, collectors of both fine art and folkcraft. On the left, the two-piece chest was both staircase and storage area in a traditional house. The chest at the right, a small kitchen *tansu,* is topped by a 6th-7th century *haniwa* figure of a wild boar from a noble's tomb.

Flanking the couch are a merchant's document chest from Tohoku (northern Japan) and a *hibachi* or brazier for making tea and heating saké.

The Arons replace their paintings and scrolls every month with those stored since Mrs. Aron says, "It would be a shame to have them damaged in a short time here in Manhattan when they have survived hundreds of years in Japan." The window treatment helps protect them since the shades combine Mylar with a material that blocks damaging ultraviolet light. Mark Hampton designed the setting for the Aron's changing collection.

all. They were once common in homes, storehouses and shops to provide access to an upper story. With storage space always at a premium, the drawers under the steps were a practical solution. These freestanding pieces, usually lightweight in construction, are becoming increasingly scarce.

What constitutes an antique chest? According to experts Ty and Kiyoko Heineken, a chest has to pre-date the end of the Meiji period, 1912. Its value increases if its structural wood, hardware, hinged doors and sliding-door frame are original. The original finish or a refinish precisely like the first is preferable. The use of polyurethane or oil-base stains, the Heinekens explain in their book *Tansu,* destroys the antique's value.

Judging a chest's origin is tricky business and is dependent on a variety of factors, including such features as joinery, choice of woods, and subtleties in the hardware. In general, a chest with a locking bar over the drawers is older than one with individually locked drawers.

Chests should be purchased from a reputable dealer if the goal is an authentic antique. If, however, the search is simply for a chest with character, there is more flexibility in

Far left: Lisbeth and Carter Beise bought a portion of a staircase chest to house their stereo equipment and adapted it to fit their apartment. An antique obi cascades towards the Japanese birdcage, whose stone bird subsists on potpourri. A Japanese bamboo pillow rests on an antique Korean wedding chest now filled with compact discs.

▼ Staircase chests create a unique look placed back-to-back in the home of Carol and Lieutenant General J.B. Davis, USAF. The dolls displayed on one of the steps are from an outdoor market in Japan, as is the temple lantern which has been electrified.

The Oriental carpet was a gift of the Japanese government to General Douglas MacArthur for his Yokohama command office after World War II. It is now part of the furnishings of the residence of the Commander in Chief of the U.S. Armed Forces in Japan, currently General Davis.

▼ *On the preceding page and below:* Massive kitchen chests *(mizuya-dansu)* are effortlessly accommodated in the Puget Sound home of Kim and George Suyama. Both chests repeat the built-in positions they held in the traditional Japanese house. Behind each painting is additional space. Mr. Suyama, a Seattle architect, has mounted the art on hanging sliders that conceal an elaborate entertainment system. Artists are Joseph Goldberg (previous page) and Alden Mason, both residents of the Northwest. The ash dining table on the previous page is Mr. Suyama's design. Wooden peg construction makes it easy to dismantle.

shopping. New *tansu* are still being made in Japan by master craftsman who have inherited the patient techniques of their forebears. Whatever the choice, even though the chest has been built with climatic changes in mind, it is a good idea to use a humidifier in a dry climate to keep the interior wood and backboards from splitting.

One contemporary cabinet maker in Sendai, Hiroshi Kumano, sees his work as a means of saving the

▼ Varying the chest-on-chest format, Tosh and Robert Beeman have separated a kitchen *tansu* to achieve a built-in look for their dining room. Their sprawling ranch in California's wine country shows strong architectural connections with Japan, Mrs. Beeman's ancestral home.

human race. Patricia Massy, crafts journalist, reports his position in The Japan Times: "What causes war? Greed. But if you have one beautiful *tansu* you needn't another. You will feel an aura of contentment as you gaze at its deep lacquer and its beautiful proportions. So I say missiles will not bring peace and happiness, but *tansu* will."

▼ The Seattle condominium of designer Paula Devon Raso reveals her eclectic spirit. A small chest *(ko-dansu)* for documents and small items, made of paulownia wood, circa 1920, rests on a French garden bench. Appointments include 19th century Italian lanterns and mirror, an equally old French candelabra, and shopkeeper stools from China. From Japan are obi pillows backed with silk plus lacquered food boxes, once a gift from Cole Porter to actress Ina Claire.

▼ A plexiglass table frames a Meiji era Fukushima clothing chest in Renée and Dan Kubiak's Tokyo apartment.

The 100-year-old wooden palace doll *(gosho-ningyo)* derives its lustre from 30-40 layers of paint made from powdered oyster shell. During the Edo era, the dolls were given to *daimyō* (lords) when they paid their respects to the emperor in Kyoto. The dolls became widely popular and came to represent a wish for both happiness and health.

New Perspectives

Sometimes the most pleasing features of a room are a consequence of breaking the rules, of daring to look at a piece from a completely different angle. The objects shown in this chapter are generally found in other positions, roles, or contexts. Their owners, however, took unexpected approaches as they incorporated them into their lifestyles. The photos demonstrate the effectiveness of cultivating an unconventional eye.

▶ Fashion designer Mary McFadden, an avid collector of dramatic artifacts ever since her days as a journalist in South Africa, decided to turn her Manhattan *pied à terre* into a gilded jewel box. The walls, ceiling and structural column of her high rise apartment have been hand-stenciled in gold with Mogul palace designs. Presiding over the living room is a lacquered Edo period kimono stand swagged with antique fabric. An obi spans the sectional and complements the Japanese and Chinese lacquerware. The musical instrument and silver flask are from Turkey; the vertical wood carving, from Madagascar.

▶ French designer Lisbeth Beise has made two small speakers ornamental by capping them with lacquered trays in her Tokyo apartment.

Mrs. Beise acquired both the stone slab and the little feet at a demolition site — one of her favorite sources for inspiration materials. The chairs are Brazilian reproductions of classic transatlantic deck chairs. The arrangement underscores the oil by contemporary artist Fang, whose work in itself is a total East-West fusion. His compositional liberties derive from his Chinese heritage, his techniques from his Japanese master, and his themes from his Brazilian home.

▼ Making a visual pun, Mrs. Beise drapes a Brazilian fish trap lamp with a Children's Day carp, obi cords and a paper fan, while a wooden fish from a hearth hook enjoys its mirrored reflection. The antique pot is a Brazilian water jug.

▼ Mrs. Beise personalizes neutral upholstery by wrapping pillows in *yukata* remnants and an ottoman in a ragweave obi. The Brazilian lion is part of the couple's collection of folk art animals, a menagerie that Mrs. Beise says gets complicated because of the family's tendency to choose almost lifesize creatures. However, she has found that "favorite pieces seem to find a home wherever you go."

▲ An antique door makes a spacious desk for antique dealers Jeff Cline and Bill Knospe in their shop, Kagedo, in Seattle. Rich cypress sliders like this often closed off the kitchen area in old homes. In general, they are too small to use as doors in Western settings unless they are mounted in a larger frame.

Kagedo carries a wide variety of Japanese art and antiques. One of their specialties is ceramics, some of which can be seen on the counter. Left to right are: an 18th century

Karatsu ware storage jar for green tea leaves; a Korean Silla dynasty (313-668 A.D.) jar for water storage which was unearthed during the building of an airfield in the 1950's; an Edo period Tokoname ware ship's saké bottle with a heavily weighted bottom; a 16th century Bizen ware water container for use in the tea ceremony; a 19th century Koda ware *kashi-bachi* (cake container) for use in Omote Senke tea ceremony; and an early Meiji era copper *teaburi* (handwarmer).

▲ John Adair, banker turned antique dealer, has made a dining table in Tokyo out of a 150-year-old door. The door is from a *kura,* the fire resistant storehouse that held all of a family's treasures, real as well as sentimental.

The *kura,* which often stood a distance from the main house, had heavy doors to discourage thieves. Objects displayed in the main house were continuously rotated through the storehouse, according to season and occasion. Many delicate objects purchased in Japan today still come in sturdy wooden boxes so they can be put away most of the year.

An important detail in this room is the well under the table to accommodate Western guests. The antique chest on the right is a miniature bridal chest from Yamagata, while the floor lamp is one-of-a kind in wrought iron by the 20th century potter Rosanjin.

▶ A *ranma*, the horizontal wooden transom above interior partitions, is often mounted on a wall by Westerners who admire its hand-carved designs. Carol Davis found two matching geometric *ranma* at a shrine sale and hinged them vertically to serve as a backdrop for a collection of Oriental baskets. A handwoven, antique obi is swagged on a bamboo rod.

▼ An early 20th century cedar *ranma,* with the naturalistic appeal of driftwood, has been mounted in a cypress frame. Antique dealers Barbara and Robert Kehoe turned it into a sofa table for their home with a wrought-iron stand of their own design.

◄ A three-foot teaching abacus *(soroban)* rests atop a stairwell in the Tokyo studio of antique dealer Kenji Tsuchisawa. In former times, children learned how to compute with oversize versions like this which hung on classroom walls. This 60-year-old model, framed in cedar, has zelkova beads mounted on slender brushes instead of smooth rods, so the beads will stay in place when the abacus is vertical. An Indonesian *ikat* tapestry repeats the geometrics.

▼ Artful, graceful . . . and a pun. Colette and René Flipo's subway poster says, "Please don't spit on the platform." However, since "spit" and "camellia" are the same word in Japanese, *tsubaki,* the word isn't written and the flower says it all. The fresh-faced Fo Dog says "ditto." These lion dogs, *shishi,* originated with the Chinese who wanted to duplicate the stone lions that stood guard outside Buddhist temples in India. Since lions were unknown in China, the artists modeled their temple guardians after the court dog, the Pekinese pug. The black and white graphics are sumo rankings.

▶ A *kotatsu* table turned on its side awaits visitors to Carol and J.B. Davis's Yokota Air Force Base home. Such tables exhibit impressive craftsmanship since the lattice work is not simply an overlay. Each slat of wood is threaded through each crosspiece. The *kotatsu* is an antique design created to provide a framework over a small hearth in the floor. When covered with a quilt, family and friends can sit with their legs under the quilt for warmth. These tables are still in use today, modernized with electric heaters to serve as cozy conversation centers.

▼ Having placed a *kotatsu* on end for a tall table (above), it was a short step to the next Davis innovation: turning a *kotatsu* table top diagonally. Carol Davis ingeniously breaks a long expanse of glass in a sun room with a *kotatsu*/trellis suspended on a chain. The grid filters the sun, while the wood softens the severity of the glass.

An unusual rectangular *kotatsu* grid becomes a three-way table in the Tokyo studio of Kenji Tsuchisawa, owner of Okura Oriental Art. These latticed low tables come in many sizes, but are generally square. This one, made of *hinoki* (Japanese cypress) and about 50 years old, must have been commissioned for a large family. Mr. Tsuchisawa removed its legs and attached ready-made supports from a hardware store. Since the new legs are made of two interlocking sections of different lengths, the table can be converted to a coffee table or lowered further to its original height for floor-seated dining.

◀ *Shōji* window panels are an obvious accompaniment to Japanese pieces. They are not so obvious a choice for an Art Déco family room. Yet Kathleen and Michael Sparer have succeeded in translating the concept into an Art Déco design that pulls the whole room together. Screen maker, Brian Consterdine, owner of Design *Shōji*, reports that these wood and fiberglass *shōji* in many different designs are becoming increasingly popular to soften the large amounts of glass used in California homes.

The room's theme was inspired by the 1930's furniture from a movie theater executive's office, and the rug was custom-designed to coordinate.

The Spirit of Bamboo

As a plant and as a medium, bamboo has a colorful heritage in Asia. Man's most useful plant, it binds the soil against flood and earthquake, provides a crisp food in its young shoots, and serves literally thousands of daily purposes with its incredibly strong yet resilient culms. From skyscraper scaffolding to home construction, from weapons to medicine, from musical instruments to kitchen tools, bamboo has been extensively utilized through the ages. Today, bamboo objects in the home provide another link with nature, another opportunity to resist the synthetic. Whether the choice is a signed basket or a country craft, the selection is a pleasant understatement.

Bamboo baskets are a study in themselves and span a spectrum of styles from humble to regal. Japan is the only culture in the world to develop bamboo weaving purely as an art form. A newcomer to the world of Japanese antiques often wonders how a basket can cost $1,500 or $3,000 or even $5,000. The high-priced baskets are usually one-of-a-kind creations signed by

▲ On a misty day, the view from the living room of Reiko and Yoshihiro Takishita's 250-year-old home in the hills of Kamakura looks like a modern silkscreen. The bamboo is *moso,* the world's largest variety, which can reach 12" in diameter. Flanking the door are an Edo period merchant's chest *(tansu)* with a Meiji era basket, an 18th century bronze temple candlestick, and a Sendai chest, also Meiji, topped by a late Edo lantern that burned camellia oil.

▶ A classic basket of split bamboo from the golden age of Japanese basket weaving, the Meiji era, graces the Takishita home in Kamakura. Derived from Chinese designs, it is tightly woven to resemble a bronze urn. The two-panel screen depicting bamboo is from the same period.

master weavers. Only a handful of these recognized masters are working today, and their contemporary pieces have been known to sell for tens of thousands of dollars. Older baskets can still be acquired for less than $2,000.

The art, evolving from utilitarian baskets of daily life, became refined in the 16th century with the development of the tea ceremony. This ritual called for the appreciation of a flower arrangement placed in a basket in the *tokonoma* (display alcove) of the main room. Early art baskets were extremely elegant, imitating symmetrical Chinese baskets made with thin strips of bamboo. Tea master Sen no Rikyu (1522-91) eventually brought rustic

◀ Field flowers restore life to this 19th century bamboo *ikebana* basket from Tochigi Prefecture in Erika and Peter Aron's Manhattan home.

In the foreground is a carpenter's tool for marking straight lines, a *sumi-tsubo* or an ink-line reel. Cotton cord from the reel passed through a recess that held inked padding. The line was pulled through and then snapped like a modern chalk-line across a board. Often made of beautifully grained *keyaki,* and sometimes ornately carved, the tools were status symbols in their day and are now collectors' items.

▼ Antique baskets, like this Meiji era free-form design, can be cleaned with a small brush, but never with water which would destroy the patina of age.

▼ The lacquered birdcage, about 140 years old, is crafted of resilient bamboo, split as fine as wire. It accents the guest room of June Laben, whose Connecticut gallery, The Kura, specializes in fine antiques. Under the Mori woodblock print of a woman at her toilette is an Edo period lacquered hand mirror with its own stand. The temple candlestick is over 120 years old.

containers back into favor, and basket makers turned to more relaxed, spontaneous designs using thicker strips of bamboo. During the Edo era (1603-1868), the refined Chinese style became popular again among the *daimyō* (feudal lords), but with a distinctly Japanese asymmetrical turn. As the merchant class took up the tea ceremony and

▶ Best-selling novelist Eric V. Lustbader spends a great deal of time mentally plunged into the exotic world of samurai and ninja. He and his wife Victoria, an editor, enjoy the contrast of a few carefully chosen Japanese art objects against the lines of their soaring contemporary home on eastern Long Island. Two antique split-bamboo baskets and an 18th century Buddha link their living room, designed by Eugénie Au Kim, to ancient Japan. The coffee table, hand-rubbed lacquer, is a signed piece. A close-up of one of the baskets is on the previous page.

began to rival the *daimyō* in elegance, there was a great demand for new shapes, and craftsmen began to sign their works.

Basket weaving as an art form reached its peak in the Meiji and Taisho periods (1868-1926). The quality of baskets of this era was unsurpassed and represents the culmination of 350 years of weaving.

Japanese basket makers have always had a ready source of material since over half of the world's 1,000 species of bamboo are found in Japan, ranging in size from plant grasses to giant size stalks 120 feet tall and a foot in diameter. New residents in the Orient soon learn to appreciate the gentle rustle of bamboo in the garden; they are less

prepared for its phenomenal growth. A sprout emerges in full diameter with all its joints visible and reaches full height in 60 to 90 days. This means that a two-inch shoot in the spring will be fluttering against a second story window in August. There is a documented instance in Kyoto of bamboo growing four feet in a single day.

Primitive people often thought the flowering of bamboo presaged disaster. Depending on the species, bamboo will flower only every 30, 60 or even 120 years. And when it flowers, it dies. All plants of the species die simultaneously wherever it is found in the world — a drama

▲ Designer Lisbeth Beise covered a hardware store tension rod with bamboo, split lengthwise, to hold a *haori* which is turned inside out. The same technique was used for the paper shades. Another length of bamboo has been added on the right counter for decorative balance.

that bewildered those who were unaware of the cycle.

Bamboo has been memorialized by painters and poets through the ages in the East. A symbol of endurance, bending but never breaking in the snow, it is one of the "Three Friends of Winter" along with the pine and the plum tree. Pine needles and bamboo leaves remain green all winter, while the plum blooms in February, sometimes in the snow. Eight hundred years ago, the Chinese poet Pou Sou-tung wrote: "A meal should have meat, but a house must have bamboo. Without meat we become thin; without bamboo we lose serenity and culture itself."

▲ A field worker's rugged bamboo backpack purchased in Kyushu, the southernmost of Japan's four main islands, is put to more delicate service in Doris and David Luening's suburban New York master bath. The rustic chair is a family piece of New England origin.

▲ A row of cut bamboo becomes a backdrop as well as a sturdy retaining wall for the sunken Japanese garden bordering Eric Lustbader's deck.

▶ The Oriental touch sets apart the suburban New York home of Sue and Guy Magnuson. Their fans survive the rigors of winter and the summer sun, proving the strength of the splayed bamboo frames and the durability of handmade paper. Called Muragame fans, after the city in Kagawa Prefecture where they are still handmade as commemorative items, the fans were acquired during the Magnusons' years in the Far East. They have become symbolic of Mrs. Magnuson's business, Eastern Dreams, which specializes in home accessories from many Asian countries.

◀ Tea ceremony paper umbrellas, marvels of ingenuity and craftsmanship, become appropriate poolside furnishings at Mary Griggs Burke's Japanese-inspired home outside New York City. Umbrella artisans in Gifu City near Nagoya still practice the time-consuming craft, shaping the delicate bamboo frames by hand and coating the handmade papers with persimmon juice for extra durability.

▲ Bamboo of varying sizes performs utilitarian service as fence, curb and blinds at this 20th century home in Japan.

◀ Bamboo, a natural conduit, channels rain spill from a hill to keep this welcoming water basin full.

▼ Per Schmølcher, art director of two Takashimaya department stores, likes to take friends picnicking at Mt. Takao. His choice of fresh, green bamboo as food containers is as practical as it is inviting. The sturdy culms protect the food, are biodegradable, and as the ancients knew, provide a natural preservative. Since the Middle Ages, bamboo has also been used as an antidote to poison. According to recent research, bamboo has been found to hold a natural silica that absorbs toxic agents.

The festive lights were inspired by parties in Mr. Schmølcher's native Denmark where candles shaded with paper are placed in the snow to greet guests. Here a length of bamboo has been topped with a cone of Japanese handmade paper. The squares of silk tied around the bamboo are party favors. Mr. Schmølcher designed the translucent mesh umbrella that dapples the picnic with shadows.

▶ Mr. Schmølcher, author of *Table Talk,* a photographic tour of dining celebrations, uses split, green bamboo at a Tokyo cocktail party not only as a conversation piece, but as a useful server, seemingly molded to fit a variety of canapes. It was once widely believed that keeping wine in green bamboo for a few days improved its flavor.

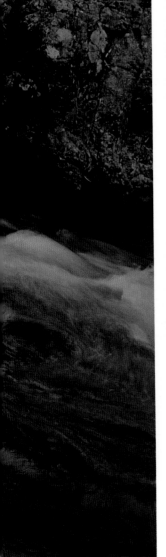

Room
to Vary

The West calls it "open landscape" — an interior design plan based on partial, movable walls. The Japanese simply call it home, since flexible space has been an integral part of Japanese daily life for centuries. The walls of the traditional house are movable and even removable, accommodating changes in activity, weather and number of occupants.

The phrase "my room" was non-existent in old Japan since any room could be adapted for sleeping, eating, working or entertaining. Partial walls, sliding doors, screens and hanging fabric defined interior space. Removable *shōji*, bamboo blinds (*sudare*), and doorway curtains (*noren*) marked flexible exterior lines. When this concept is applied to contemporary rooms with the aid of Japanese elements, the amalgam is both imaginative and practical.

▶ California designer Chadine has turned the predictable proportions of an American bedroom into an unexpected Japanese retreat. The *tatami* mat platform, made of Douglas fir, can be easily dismantled. Placed asymmetrically, the golden, antique folding screen (*byōbu*), in its classic position opposite windows, brightens the room with reflected light by day and provides a cozy wall at night.

Aristocratic and samurai families often commissioned screens for special occasions. Auspicious cranes and turtles were painted in monochrome ink at the birth of a child; other celebrations called for gold leaf.

◀ Custom-made queen size *futon* and cushions, plus four *tatami* mats edged by a wooden trim, turn half of a tiny room into a combination guest room/TV corner. The covered tea boxes become the headboard at night, while the straw snowshoe holding champagne awaits guests at Lisbeth and Carter Beise's Tokyo apartment. *Sudare*, thin bamboo blinds, unroll for privacy. They were used on the verandas of temples and traditional houses.

▲ Acting on the Japanese concept that things should be slowly discovered rather than immediately apparent, Australians Ann and Chris Seddon have used *sudare* as a subtle room divider in their Tokyo home. Mrs. Seddon, artist and author, and Mr. Seddon, an architect, combine their eclectic tastes harmoniously with the juxtaposition, among other things, of a David Hockney print, Victorian drawings and a Chinese scroll.

▲ Normally, a six-panel, antique screen would pose positioning problems in a small apartment. Seattle designer Paula Devon Raso was undaunted. She not only succeeds, she has it serve double duty, since the end panel closes off a secondary entrance to the kitchen.

Ms. Raso has always been drawn to Japanese pieces because they mix so well with other antiques. The Edo period screen seems a natural companion for the other 18th century pieces: a French candlestick lamp and country armoire, Biedermeier chairs, and Chinese porcelain. Ms. Raso had the stand built for the red lacquered Japanese box. Also Japanese are the black lacquered box on the desk; the brass hand mirror; and the grinning Hotei, one of the Seven Gods of Good Fortune. The flooring is Tarkette, a European tongue-in-groove pre-finished floor that floats over sound-proofing foam.

▲ The low *shōji* screens of a teahouse have been adapted to form a room divider in Colette and René Flipo's Tokyo apartment. The room exemplifies the Japanese concept of *shibui* — the power of quietness and understatement, especially in commonplace things, to create beauty. The quality of *shibui* invites prolonged examination, never revealing itself all at once. The finely lacquered nesting boxes are 20th century *obento* boxes (for food). The antique camp chair is South African, as is the stool, carved from a single piece of wood. The pillows and blanket are Mexican.

▼ A series of custom-made *shōji* provide maximum flexibility in the entryway of a condominium on the San Francisco peninsula. For a large party, the doors slide away to reveal a Japanese design theme throughout the apartment. In order to create a courtyard effect for her client, Lequita Vance-Watkins, Carmel designer (and haiku poet), combined Peblon flooring with a prefab wood veneer. A bamboo screen has been mounted on the front door. The *shōji* were made by Henry Nakata of San Jose.

▶ Seattle architect George Suyama's home on the edge of Puget Sound embodies the concept of free-flowing living space with a minimum of fixed walls. The *sudare* surrounding the sleeping area re-define the size and light in the master bedroom. An antique, cotton wedding *futonji* (quilt cover) serves as the bed covering. (See page 95 for an explanation of its design and the *tsutsugaki* dye process.)

Outdoor View

Why do so many first time visitors to Japan — even those with no interest in trees or flowers — suddenly fall in love with the gardens? The answer goes well beyond aesthetics to a highly developed tradition of subtle communication that emanates calm.

To the Japanese, gardens are vital lifelines to mental refreshment. Partly because the country is so crowded — 80% of the population lives on 3% of the land — the Japanese find it essential to have a ready link with nature. Even in Tokyo where the eye can be exhausted by the riot of neon, concrete and metal, it is easy to find tranquil retreats.

But more profoundly, whether the escape is a narrow strip of earth along a property line or one of the nation's three most famous landscape gardens,* all Japanese gardens convey spiritual and philosophical messages. All are designed with the essential cultural understanding that man and nature are one and all aim to express the religious belief that the whole universe is contained in its smallest part.

Buddhism teaches that everything in the world, right down to the smallest seed, is governed by the same cosmic forces. The highly stylized pruning that characterizes the gardens is an attempt to emphasize the essential qualities of each tree and bush, whether it is the gnarled

*Kenrokuen in Kanazawa City, Kairakuen in Ibaraki Prefecture and Korakuen outside of Okayama.

◀ A traditional Japanese room, often referred to as a *tatami* room because of its straw floor covering, ideally should have a garden view. Eric V. Lustbader, author of *French Kiss* and *White Ninja,* has created a *tatami* retreat in his home that makes the garden seem an integral part of the interior. Three dwarf cut-leaf maples — Coral Bark, Waterfall and Butterfly — provide a sampling of colors year round for the classical Japanese pursuit of maple viewing.

▼ Outside the room, a simulated river meanders through low plantings and under the bridge, which is a wood and granite bench designed by Michael Ince of Amagansett, N.Y.

The components of a Japanese garden are supposed to receive more than an occasional glance. They are continual "companions" of the residents, and are necessarily low to be seen by people sitting on the floor.

branches of a juniper or the graceful shoots of a stand of bamboo. From a practical standpoint, the careful pruning allows the sun to reach the lower branches. But the pruning is intended only to suggest the overall shapes which the mind must complete, just as the meaning of abstract Zen gardens lies only in the mind of the viewer.

A private Japanese garden is not an isolated entity. It is designed to be an integral part of the house and extension of the interior, not a garnish around the foundation line. The courtyard garden is usually combined with a special *shōji* wall designed to bring nature indoors. One expert on traditional architecture, Teiji Itoh, delights in describing the area found under the eaves of the old houses. He says that architects consider this space the interior while gardeners call it the exterior. "This is a difficult concept for Western minds for whom a thing must be either A or B. Here it is at once two things without being either."

▲ A Kasuga lantern, named after the Nara shrine where the style originated, helps make a small border edging John Wisner's New York driveway memorable.

▶ A California stone yard yielded the water basin that has been combined with pebbles, volcanic rocks and low plantings by David H. Engel, considered by many the dean of Japanese garden design in the U.S. The garden transforms the deck of Mr. Wisner's Long Island summer home.

60

Because these intimate gardens are on continuous view through the seasons, they are not supposed to change drastically during the year, since the changing colors of large banks of flowers are considered disturbing to those within. The scene is to be admired for its line and mass, accomplished largely through the use of steadfast evergreens and rock, which are revered for their longevity. Picture perfect rocks aren't simply fortuitous finds on garden sites. Rocks can be purchased for hefty prices, and for centuries have been moved across Japan for landscapers. In the 16th century, General Hideyoshi's armies often looted prize stones from the gardens of the vanquished and sent them home wrapped in silk. Water, too, is another basic element, but is sometimes simulated with pebbles or raked sand.

Through careful framing of space and manipulation of scale, Japanese gardeners are unrivalled at creating

▲ Grass circles suggesting giant stepping stones lead visitors to the country home of Mary Griggs Burke, who built an open plan house in 1954 to "keep in touch with the beautiful natural surroundings" of her Long Island site. Mrs. Burke's grounds were landscaped in the Japanese spirit after her first visit to Japan and a tour of its important gardens. The "stones" were inspired by the giant circles of moss in white sand at the Sambo-in Temple in Kyoto. The construction project launched Mrs. Burke on a lifelong study of Japanese culture and art, during which she has acquired one of America's most important collections of Japanese art.

◀ True to the Japanese design spirit, the stone basin is partially hidden by the black pine. In Japanese gardens, objects are supposed to be discovered one by one rather than be visible from afar. This concept is applicable even in small areas.

the illusion of spaciousness. Sometimes a private garden blocks out an unpleasant view. At other times, it capitalizes on distant scenery by ingenious design techniques that enlarge the immediate space. Whatever its goal, it never reveals itself all at once. Symmetry is rejected as too predictable; it offers no mystery. Straight paths are also avoided because it is believed that evil follows straight lines.

Zen gardens in particular are designed for meditation. In the Zen sect of Buddhism, truth is acquired not through scriptures or teachings, but in sudden bursts of insight which can be triggered by anything — a darting fish, the sound of the wind, even a group of rocks. Zen monks attempt to contemplate nothingness for days seeking an inner quiet. Their spare, unchanging gardens become aids to stimulate enlightenment.

Lanterns

One garden ornament of immediate universal appeal is the stone lantern, *ishi-dōrō*. Imported with Buddhism from India by way of China, lanterns originated on temple grounds to hold fire, a sacred symbol of life, and were initially large and ornate. Sen no Rikyu, the innovative 16th century tea master, decided to use lanterns in his teahouse gardens since he liked their gentle light for evening tea ceremonies. He created simple designs in keeping with his

▲ Some lanterns are designed with broad tops to catch mounds of snow. This one, brought from Tokyo, is at home in the rugged landscape of Susan and Steven Geffen's New York property.

▶ A few well chosen natural elements can suggest a larger garden even on a small scale. On the Flipo's Tokyo terrace, an antique brazier *(hibachi)* holds goldfish under the shade of a modern carved stone lantern.

preference for humble craftsmanship, assembling some from uncut stones, and he encouraged people to make their own. The tea garden prepares the visitor for the spiritual experience of the tea ceremony where humility is supposed to bring serenity. Anxiety and worldly cares are shed passing through the garden. Eventually, the lantern became an ornament in residential gardens and later, by strategic positioning, became a key element in drawing the visitor's eye to scenery beyond the garden.

Of the many different lantern designs seen today, the most popular is the snow-viewing lantern, *yuki-mi-dōrō*, recognized by its wide-brimmed roof designed to collect a deep pile of snow. A lantern with a hexagonal top, *hakkaku-dōrō*, is usually located at the crossroads of paths, since it casts light in several directions. Others take their names from the shrines where they originated, like the Kasuga and the Nigatsu-dokata, named after two shrines in Nara.

Every lantern is composed of five parts, originally five basic shapes meant to symbolize the five elements of the universe in ancient Japanese cosmology — sky, wind, fire, water and earth. In a Western garden, an ornamental lantern can be readily placed in a spot that might need light such as a path or a gateway, or at the edge of a pond lighting an imaginary boat landing. A flat rock underneath makes a stable base.

▲ Through the seasons, an untraditional lantern stands ready for visitors at the home of John Wisner, a New Yorker whose lifelong interest in the Far East led to his design of a Japanese-inspired house. (See page 163.) The lantern originated in San Francisco.

◄ A snow-viewing lantern waits out the rain at the Connecticut home of June Laben.

Water Basins

Another picturesque garden ornament is the stone water basin, *tsukubai,* with its bamboo dipper, *hishaku,* for washing hands and drinking in a purification ritual before the tea ceremony. Large cut stone basins are found outside temples for the same purpose. In the classic garden, the basins are either hollowed out by an artisan or are naturally formed by a waterfall, but reproductions cast in concrete are

Jauntily perched in a remote valley in New York's Catskills, improvised lanterns and an eroded stone "water basin" have delighted generations of the Tison family and their friends since the turn of the century. The house itself, now the summer home of Helen Tison Caskey, can be seen on page 138.

Its first owner, Alexander Tison, taught law at the University of Tokyo from 1889-1894, and decided on his return to the U.S. to create his own Japanese garden. Since his local Japanese gardeners didn't have access to cut stones, they used rocks from the nearby creek to provide several lanterns for the grounds.

readily available. Originally, taller versions were for nobility, but the tea ceremony abolished this distinction and both aristocrat and commoner must bend in equality.

Often a small bamboo pipe supplies a steady stream of water to the basin. (See page 47.) When the pipe is rigged to a seesaw piece of bamboo that fills with water, tilts, empties itself, and then tilts again with a clap on a rock, the device is called *shishi-odoshi*. The hollow sound, occurring about every two minutes, is very pleasing to Japanese garden enthusiasts, but the device was created centuries ago to scare wild boars away from the vegetation

◀ A ritual water basin with its cherry bark dipper, a tradition in tea gardens, is paired with a flowering quince to decorate a picnic lunch on a Tokyo terrace. The grass growing at the base of the plant is health food for the owner's cats. The cloth is a carrying cloth, a *furoshiki*, printed with a design by Hiroshige. Plates are summer soba dishes.

▼ Even a view of Central Park can be improved with a small Japanese border garden that knows no season. Designer Sam Takeuchi softened the stone parapet of his client's balcony with plantings. (See page 131.)

near mountain streams. Eventually it was used in gardens to discourage deer and birds.

Most gardens are considered at their best when wet with dew or half dry from a rain. Moisture is particularly desirable on a summer evening for cooling adjacent rooms. Today as in the former times, the front garden and the courtyard are often sprinkled with water to provide a hospitable welcome for guests.

◄ Rain spilling from the roof becomes a thing of beauty. While the West conceals it in metal pipes, the Japanese enjoy watching it cascade down a rainchain. Often the chain is strung with small cups like the one Chadine Flood Gong found in a San Francisco antique store to help transform the modern lines of her California home. The grove of black bamboo has its lower branches trimmed. New canes are green the first year, speckled brown in the second, and completely black by the third.

◄ A rainchain and its catch basin at the Ryo Daishi Temple in Tokyo make a refreshing vignette even after the rain has stopped.

▲ A carefully selected flat rock serves as a viewing platform for Mrs. Burke's lotus pond. Slightly cantilevered over the water, it naturally bridges a spillway that runs across the property carrying the cooling overflow.

◀ Looking down from the Lustbader deck, the viewer's eye is drawn from the pool to the Japanese-inspired garden by Charlie Marder of Bridgehampton, which borrows magnitude from the mass of pitch pine native to Eastern Long Island.

Dining Presentations

▲ San Francisco porcelain dealer Emily Newell has a natural affinity for Asian themes having grown up in Hong Kong and Singapore. Using many of the items from her shop, Oriental Porcelain Gallery, she has created a festive holiday table combining Imari bowls and soba cups, Kutani sashimi dishes — all Edo period — with modern lacquerware and chopstick rests. The wine bottle stands in a smoker's porcelain *hibachi* (brazier), nestled in a lacquered *haizen* for washing saké cups. The table itself is a *kotatsu* raised to Western dining height by the antique shop, The Crane and The Turtle, San Francisco. (The original function of the *sumi-tsubo* holding the flowers is explained on page 41.)

▶ The Manhattan skyline seems to be a made-to-order backdrop for Alice and Halsey North's bold collection of contemporary ceramics. As arts management consultants and leaders of craft tours to Japan for New York's Japan Society, the Norths have the opportunity to find the best in the dynamic field of ceramics in both Japan and the United States. Japanese ceramic artists are working within a 10,000-year tradition, yet stand at the forefront of modern art, inspiring potters around the world.

Detroiter Mary Roehm is a pioneer of American wood-fired ceramics. Her saké cups and serving bowl are on the table; two wood-fired porcelain teapots, on the ledge.

Shiro Otani, who works in wood-fired earthenware with Shigaraki clay, made the saké bottle at the left place setting and the pot in the window with the "bull's eye." New Yorker Jeff Shapiro, who teaches the art he learned in Bizen, Japan, created the other saké bottle and the pot to the left of the "bull's eye." Mashiko, the potter's village near Nikko, is represented by Tatsuzō Shimaoka, whose deep blue, salt-glazed vessel stands third from right.

Other well-known potters are Yoshikane Matsubayashi, 15th generation Asashi potter from Uji (small bowls on table); Rob Barnard, a Virginia potter who studied in Shigaraki (far left pot); Cynthia Bringle, potter and long-time resident at Penland School of Crafts in North Carolina (three plates); and Nancee Meeker from Rhinecliff, N.Y., whose carved and pitfired pot is left of the teapots.

▼ Yann Beise's eighth birthday party pops with East-West ideas. Inflatable paper balls form the centerpiece on the *washi* and tissue paper tablecloth. Origami squares become coasters; licorice decorates the stemware. The planes swooping low with place cards and the carp party bags come from the Asakusabashi section of Tokyo. The Japanese woodblock prints serving as placemats are party favors, protected by sheets of acrylic.

▼ Easter comes to the Kubiak family's Tokyo table. Part of daughter Erin's collection of fans and bunnies sets the East-West theme. Chopsticks are bound with gift-wrapping cord, *mizuhiki,* to hold sprigs of stock. The cascading centerpiece comes from a lantern store in Asakusabashi.

▲ Home fashion designer Naomi Iwasaki Hoff adds splashes of color to a Tokyo dining table with silk brocade placemats and napkin rings that she created from an antique kimono. The lacquered bowls are also antique; table and chairs, contemporary Italian. The art is an original Yoshito Takahashi painting on handmade paper he calls *"mashi."*

▲ Thai cookbook author Puangkram Schmitz teams Imari serving bowls with Thai stoneware and cutlery. Her low profile centerpiece utilizes a shallow container designed to display a *bonsai* tree, but also doubles on occasions as a serving dish. The fresh flowers lie in a very shallow pool of water — an arrangement readily duplicated by the most harried hostess.

Rosemarie and Leighton Longhi renovated their Fifth Avenue, New York apartment to allow them to enjoy some of the world's finest pieces of Japanese art. Their home is also a changing gallery since Mr. Longhi, a dealer in Japanese art, acquires pieces for museums and corporate collections around the world. The Longhis' philosophy on living with art corresponds to that of the Japanese who do not allow paintings and art to compete with each other. Instead, items appropriate for the occasion or season are brought out of storage for temporary display.

Recesses in the dining room walls provide a ready showcase. The six-panel screen can be changed in minutes and is lit with soft lights in the ledge. Gracing this formal setting is a 17th century Kano school painting of the Twenty-Four Filial Pieties, *Nijūshiko*. The wooden statue at the end of the room is a 13th century figure of Bishamonten, one of the four Heavenly Kings who guard Buddha's law in the four quarters of the universe.

On the Regency table, Edo period Arita porcelain is combined with Limoges service plates, Baccarat and Riedel crystal and a 19th century Japanese bamboo flower basket.

Left of the screen, a gilded wooden *koma inu*, a mythological lion/dog dating from the 14th century, sits atop a rare Ming stand. The room acquires a soft glow from the silver Japanese paper glazed with paint.

Eloquent Artifacts

Many items emerge from Japan's past that are intriguing in themselves, but carry little indication of their previous roles. Yet when the whole story is known, they become even more interesting. The artifacts shown in this chapter have come to rest in surprising new corners around the world, but a little background information is required to appreciate their rich heritage.

▲ A reproduction of a Buddhist temple drum (*mokugyo*) rests on a sill in the apartment of designer Renée Kubiak. Its hollow wood sounds a sonorous note when struck with a padded stick. Gongs shaped like fish were first used in China to announce the hours but, when introduced to Japan in the 17th century, were utilized to call priests to meals at Zen temples.

A legend explains its origin: a disciple of Buddha was punished for his failures by being turned into a fish with a tree growing out of his head. He begged Buddha to release him from his suffering by making something useful from the tree. So Buddha cut the wood into the shape of a fish and used it to announce meal time "to save all beastly persons."

▶ The aged wooden pieces on the shelves evoke the splendors of the richly decorated Buddhist temples. Capping the top shelf is one of the many different shapes that compose the intricate structure in a roof overhang. It is a *kaerumata,* or "frog-leg" strut, a functional support that evolved into an elaborate ornament in various designs. The candle holders are beam supports, while the cloud carving, *kumo-hijiki,* served as a bracket arm between supporting columns. In the foreground, the Meiji era porcelain teapot is in mint condition. When the translucent Satsuma cup is held up to the light, the face of an apprentice geisha, a *maiko,* appears at the bottom.

▶ Fish stories abound in Carol Davis's collection. Dominating the scene is the Japanese hearth hangar, a *jizai-kagi*. Designed to hold a kettle over an open fire, it was the most respected furnishing in the old farmhouse and generated many superstitions. Moving it unnecessarily was believed to bring bad luck. Playing with it — perhaps children were tempted to swing it — was said to bring financial misfortune or, if a voyage was planned, rough seas. In some districts, whenever something was lost or misplaced in the house, a strip of paper was tied to the hook and the missing object was soon discovered. Since fire was a constant fear, the hook was often ornamented with a fish, the symbol of water.

On the wall is an antique store sign, a *kanban*, advertising children's aspirin. The large fish with the ball in its mouth is another reproduction of a temple drum. The Chinese used to say that the fish shape was chosen to call Buddhist disciples from their idleness since fish never close their eyes and are on watch day and night.

▶ Hearth hooks in this shape have been traditionally nicknamed Daikoku after one of the Seven Gods of Good Fortune borrowed from the Chinese. Daikoku and Ebisu are known as "kitchen gods," patrons of farmers and fishermen and providers of household wealth. Daikoku always wears a hat with a crown, so hooks with crosspieces receive his name. Ebisu gives his name to the "J" hook shown on the opposite page.

◄ John Adair's modern-looking sculpture is a hearth hook, a *sora-kagi,* 100 to 150 years old, carved out of single piece of wood. Unlike the *jizai-kagi* pot hook which hung from an adjustable bamboo pole over the open fire, the *sora-kagi* was suspended by rope from a ceiling beam. Massive hooks, some the size of small chests, originated in Gifu, Fukui and Ishikawa and were commissioned to reflect the homeowner's wealth and position.

Mr. Adair's hook rests on a document chest, a *choba-dansu,* 150 to 200 years old, from the Kyoto region. The textile piece, however, eclipses everything else in the room in terms of collector value. This cotton quilt cover (*futonji*) for a Kyushu wedding bed depicts the Chinese lion, the ancient symbol of masculinity, and the peony, the symbol of femininity. The design was drawn by hand towards the end of the last century in the *tsutsugaki* technique. (See page 95.) Since it is in excellent condition, it is worth several thousand dollars.

A Takayama lantern sits atop a woman's clothing chest (*onna-dansu*) recognizable by its two small top drawers. The finely-grained zelkova shows Mr. Adair's careful restoration: the soot from generations of indoor cooking fires has not been totally removed around the edges of the hardware.

▶ Many visitors to Japan start collections of the astrological animal of the year of their birth. John Adair, born in Kansas in the year of the horse, was drawn to this votive painting or *ema* from Yamagata which is a distinguished example of an entire art form. In ancient times, horses were donated to shrines to accompany prayers of petition. Black horses, for example, were given in time of drought; white, in times of flood, since horses were believed to be the mounts of gods and were especially favored by the god of water.

Gradually, the live gifts were replaced by lifesize clay or wooden horses and later by paintings and woodblock prints. Sometime during the Muromachi period (1333-1573), other subjects began to appear, including the other 11 astrological animals. The *ema* became a popular votive offering with the warrior class who tried to outdo each other in finding famous artists to paint large portraits of their favorite steeds. In this 18th century *ema*, the horse is tied, since it was feared that if the mount were well rendered, it would come to life and bolt away. It is signed by the artist and the four individuals who donated it to a shrine.

The practice of donating *ema* exists today with various plaques inscribed for different petitions available at shrines for a small donation. The donor's name and date are added and the plaque is hung at the shrine.

The chest is late 19th century from Sendai and was originally built into wall cabinets in the main room of a house.

▶ Another antique *ema* of unknown vintage is a focal point in a small guestroom in a Manhattan apartment, where Sam Takeuchi's design talents have maximized his client's light and space.

◀ Twentieth century *ema* by a distinguished art restorer and teacher, Hokusai Yoshiwara, show the entire astrological menagerie. These *ema* are miniatures of those at the Five-Storied Pagoda at Nikko's Toshogu Shrine. The unusual collection was a gift to the Magnuson family from a Tokyo friend.

The 12 zodiac animals are not only said to influence the personalities of people born to their year, they also provide a handy way to determine someone's age. By asking a person's sign, age can be guessed in increments of 12. The animals are displayed here in zodiac order: mouse (1984), ox (85), tiger (86), rabbit (87), dragon (88), snake (89), horse (90), sheep (91), monkey (92), bird (93), dog (94), boar (95).

The scene is the master bath of designer John Rogers whose Long Island home, understandably named "Above It All," commands a sweeping view. His folk art lamp is a lacquered horned cask (*tsuno-daru*) used to bring saké to various celebrations. Many casks were made for engagement ceremonies when the groom sent saké to the bride's family. A kimono stand holds the towels.

◄ The latest in kitchen sinks is effectively paired in Mr. Rogers' home with a 19th century washbasin, the lacquered planter. Its elaborate gold leaf design indicates it belonged to someone of lofty rank.

▲ Another antique washbasin finds a natural setting in a Seattle powder room. It has seen generations of service to women who used it for rinsing their hair. Harmoniously blending the art of different cultures, Paula Devon Raso has added a print that belonged to her grandmother, a Chinese jar and a small doll in the *gosho-ningyō* tradition (see page 25). The architectural piece is Italian.

▲ Two elements of traditional Japan greet visitors to Amaury Saint-Gilles' Hawaiian home. The unusual basket, almost a yard wide, is a *kaiko-zaru* (silkworm basket) and dates to the turn of the century when hand-spun silk was still a cottage industry. Such baskets, suspended horizontally under the eaves of farm houses, held mulberry leaves to feed the silkworms. Mr. Saint-Gilles uses it to display his collection of *omamori*, protective talismans still sold at temples and shrines. Each brocade pouch holds a short prayer or small object to represent such petitions as good health, success in studies, easy childbirth or safe travel.

A Tokyo resident for more than two decades, Mr. Saint-Gilles founded a contemporary fine art gallery to "bridge cultures" by bringing Japanese and Western artists together. The two pieces of unglazed stoneware are those of Virginian Rob Barnard, whose work in the 15th century Yakishime wood-firing technique is greatly respected by the demanding Japanese audience.

Mr. Saint-Gilles closed his gallery in Japan in 1989 when he relocated his art interests to the "Big Island" of Hawaii, but he maintains a *pied à terre* in the mountains north of Tokyo.

▲ Interior designer and artist Doris Luening prizes a farmer's raincape, or *mino*, made of paper-thin wood shavings purchased at a folk art store in Tokyo's Ginza section. This unusual craft originates in different regions of the country and can be found in various designs and materials: rice or barley straw, reeds, shredded bark, dried seaweed and palm fiber.

Mino were often special gifts of affection between couples and are still worn in rural areas, although they are becoming increasingly scarce. The natural water-repellent silicone in the reeds causes the rain to bead and roll off. The capes remain supple for years. This one has successfully weathered the trip from Japan to the Luening home in Westchester County, New York.

Room to Dream

▶ Eugénie Au Kim makes an arresting scroll even more memorable by suspending it from the ceiling in this designer showcase room in Westhampton Beach, New York. It says "patience," and patience, she explains, is the essence of tranquility.

Ms. Au Kim, born in New York of Chinese parents, recalls that she spent a number of years trying to sort out where she belonged. She eventually realized that she did not have to embrace either culture; she could be a balance. From that point on, her design work has demonstrated smoothly integrated East/ West blends.

Viewers of the room were surprised to learn that the bed is normal Western height. The queen size mattress and the king size platform suggest the low profile of Japanese sleeping arrangements. Eli Horen, Ms. Au Kim's partner in their Southampton design company, Design Studio, swagged the windows with fabric by Boussac of France.

The floor covering is ready-made sisal, more durable than *tatami* and less expensive. The pillows are French and English tapestry textiles; the kimono, from Daikichi, Sag Harbor, N.Y.

▶Thirteen-year-old Travis Kubiak's room capitalizes on the centuries-old crafts readily available in Tokyo. The lantern and the black lacquered storage box on the desk have been personalized for Travis by artisans who are profiled in the paperback book *Kites, Crackers and Craftsmen* published in Tokyo. The lantern sports his family name; the box, his first name.

▲ A small Tokyo bedroom becomes deceptively spacious through the planning of designer Cindi Novkov, who approximates Japanese style by recessing the mattress into a floor platform. Adding to the serenity are the obi pillows by Naomi Iwasaki Hoff, the temple candlestick and the framed scrolls which say "phoenix" and "dragon." The glass base for the TV sits on a convenient turntable.

▶ Notable examples of 19th century crafts decorate John Adair's Tokyo bedroom. The wedding bed coverlet (*futonji*) bears a design that is still seen frequently on gift materials such as wrapping paper and cards. Long before the advent of commercial ribbon or cord to wrap gifts, the Japanese stretched dried abalone, *noshi*, into strands and bound them in the center to present with a gift. Since *noshi* also means "prolong" in

Japanese, the gift-giver wanted to prolong the recipient's happiness. The abalone eventually was replaced with yellow strips of paper and finally this design. This version has been created freehand in the *tsutsugaki* technique: a rice paste that resists dye is applied to fabric through a cone similar to a pastry tube. The *futonji* is early-to-mid Meiji in age, from Kurume in Kyushu.

On the wall, farm garments exemplify a rare combination of *sashiko* quilting and *kasuri* dyeing, and probably date from the Meiji era.

The sea chests flanking the bed are typical of those from Sakata in northern Yamagata Prefecture. When rice from the Yamagata paddies was shipped by boat down the Mogami River to Sakata on the Japan Sea, sea captains kept their money and documents in these sturdy *funa-dansu*.

Paula Devon Raso lets an 1880 screen create a peaceful mood in her master bedroom. The three-dimensional quality of the blossoms was achieved with gesso. The chrysanthemum is the flower of the emperor and one of Japan's favorite blooms. Antique Italian candlesticks and chair plus a small Japanese chest fill out the scene.

▲ A simple concept yields stunning results. Naomi Iwasaki Hoff took a man's antique kimono and made it into a one-of-a-kind comforter for her Tokyo apartment. The fabric's motif is of the classic Thirty-Six Immortal Poets. The contemporary lithograph is by Toko Shinoda.

▶ A small room with unusual windows becomes a distinctive guest room in Paula Devon Raso's Seattle apartment. She has accommodated the massive proportions of a Meiji era kitchen chest with the spare lines of an 1845 French campaign bed that actually folds. French doors from another structure serve as shutters. An antique *gosho* doll bids welcome. (See page 25.)

▲ In Manhattan, a 17th century screen attributed to the Kanō school dictated a bedroom's design. Given the screen as a starting point by his client, architect Sam Takeuchi built a ledge behind the headboard for its display. A wall panel above holds the upper edge in place.

The screen depicts the common theme of a powerful tiger finding shelter from a storm in a grove of bamboo. Its message — even the most powerful becomes weak in the face of nature's might. *Sumi* ink has been a favorite medium for hundreds of years in Japan to convey essences through the simplest of means.

The dragonfly on the helmet was a popular decorative motif for military pieces. Sometimes called the "victory insect," it symbolized the hope that arrows would fly directly to their targets, like the insect.

▲ *Shōji* screens have always lent themselves to endless variations. Kathleen and Michael Sparer chose an Art Déco motif to transform their California ranch house, rendering the designs in various finishes and sizes throughout the house. (See also page 37.) In the master bedroom, a blond hardwood from Malaysia called ramin has been used with fiberglass to complement the olive ash burl furniture. The walls have been glazed with brush, sponge and gauze. Etching by Sacramento artist Leslie Toms.

Ikebana: Lessons in Serenity

To the untutored eye, a Japanese flower arrangement is simply another flower arrangement. Yet that gentle spray may be the universe in miniature or a symbolic slice of life. As with so many aspects of life and art in Japan, the implied message is very important.

Sometimes only a few flowers are used. Empty space is to a floral arrangement in Japan what silence is to dialogue. Both speak volumes. Unlike Western arrangements that cluster flowers and color for dramatic effect, Japanese flower arranging — *ikebana* — seeks to harmonize line, color and container with the surrounding space. The aim is not to repeat nature, but to create a beautiful new design using several elements of nature.

The angle of the branch is generally as important as the flower, with essential angles often dictated by the style of the arrangement. Symbolism and subtle simplicity are

▶ Since there was no room on his property for a carp pond, Tokyo architect Chikafusa Sato built one into his deck, where it reflects the nearby nature sanctuary. The view from within has a focal point in the minimal arrangement of African daisies and fennel in a Meiji era, Imari platter that has been in the Sato family for three generations.

▲ Contemporary flower arrangements sometimes echo contemporary art in form, line, volume and color. This bold free-form arrangement was created to match the character of the acrylic/collage by Jude Roger, an American artist in Tokyo. The water container is behind the large rock.

constant goals. Emotion, time, place, occasion, even weather conditions can all be indicated by choice of materials and selection of angles. A bud, for example, can be used to suggest the promise of things to come. Tight buds combined with half open buds and full blown flowers imply the progression of human life. The three principal stems of some arrangements represent heaven, man and earth, and are positioned at prescribed angles. Each viewer, however, may see something different in a finished work, since arrangements are also intended to invite contemplation.

Ikebana is a contemplative pursuit, performed more for the satisfaction of expression rather than for its decorative result. One flower master calls it "an attempt to harmonize spiritual truths with material substance." As in all art, rules must be mastered before they can be abandoned in pursuit of new forms. Levels of proficiency are attained according to mastery of principles, with the student advancing to become, if interested, an accredited teacher. *Ikebana* is said to be very difficult to learn from a book, requiring continual practice and a master's on-going assessment.

For the novice, even the first lessons bring practical tips applicable to any sort of flower arranging. For example, clipping stalks under water keeps air out of the stems that would block water from rising. Japanese ingenuity has devised tricks for steadying top-heavy branches and for concealing the mechanics of support. *Ikebana* teaches how to be resourceful with backyard materials or bend a branch to suit the design.

Although *ikebana* has become largely a feminine pursuit — and in Japan is still a desirable credential in a marriage portfolio — it was strictly a masculine activity until as recently as the end of the last century. Chinese priests introduced the art to Japan in the sixth century with floral offerings to Buddha symbolizing the universe. Japanese priests taught the art to each other and to nobles through several generations. By the mid 14th century, flowers were used for hanging arrangements and shelf decorations in addition to Buddhist offerings. The priest, Senkei Ikenobo, recorded the first rules for arranging in the 15th century, thereby establishing the Ikenobo School, "using both leaves and flowers to arrange an ideal image of the inner beauty of plants." Senkei Ikenobo also contrived the first huge composition several feet tall called a *rikka* to symbolize the universe.

In the 17th century, the warrior class, the samurai, took up *ikebana* as a mental discipline, hoping to quiet their apprehensions before battle and calm their minds afterwards. They considered *ikebana* an important skill, and they built monumental arrangements to decorate their castles.

Sen no Rikyu, the 16th century tea master who simplified the tea ceremony by insisting on rustic vessels, also brought *ikebana* down to an everyday level. His arrangements for the tea ceremony specified simple designs and light colored flowers, often of only one variety, in unobtrusive containers. Sen no Rikyu captured Japan's attention by making the commonplace charming. Legends abound about his innovations. In one, he was asked by General Toyotomi Hideyoshi to make an arrangement for the general's tent where he had his tea. To Hideyoshi's delight, Sen no Rikyu collected wild flowers and using a camp bowl, positioned them delicately in a

▲ Every phase of plant life is laden with meaning in Japan. The stick-straight iris symbolizes manly integrity and its flat pointed leaves are supposed to suggest a warrior's sword. Here in a bachelor's Tokyo apartment, displayed in a lacquered kabuki makeup box, the irises are particularly appropriate. The makeup stand, more than 100 years old, belonged to a Tokyo actor. The upper section folds down into the portable box.

▲ A ceramic vessel by Marilyn Sato displays a Sogetsu arrangement of kiwi vine, banana leaf and stock. The combination of gnarled and sleek, hard and soft, dark and light represents one of the Orient's major philosophies, the harmony of complementary contrasts. In Japan, the principle is called *in* and *yo*; in China, *yin* and *yang*.

▶ Brunch at Puangkram and Fritz Schmitz's Tokyo home is sometimes set in the garden. The blossoms floating in the *hibachi* are inspired by one form of *ikebana* called *ukibana* or floating flowers. (The Japanese used to float irises in the bath to ward off disease.) A patchwork quilt underscores the colors of the Japanese and Thai dishes.

horse's bit.

By the end of the 19th century, Japanese women discovered that flower arrangements enhanced their homes and they turned to a wide variety of commonplace materials — vines, stones, shells — to make original designs.

Today, Japan has an estimated 1,000 schools of *ikebana*, while about 10 million people, mostly women, study it worldwide. Their studies generally follow one of three main schools. Classical Ikenobo School arrangements rise naturally like a tree. Their lines tend to exaggerate nature's characteristics. One of the tenets of this school is that arrangements should show an awareness of each plant's distinct, inner character.

The Ohara School, founded at the end of the 19th century, modernized *ikebana* with the introduction of the *moribana* form — an arrangement in a low dish — as opposed to the

▲ A pool of water is used in Takashi Yoshimura's freestyle arrangement of gold-banded lilies and Japanese pampas grass to convey a feeling of refreshment. Dark containers intensify reflections in the water and suggest tranquility.

◄ Toshikazu Teshima's combination of zebra grass, rose mallow and Japanese bellflower in a lacquered bamboo basket emphasizes spontaneity.

nageire, an arrangement in a tall vase, two forms that all three schools now use.

Sogetsu, or the School of the Grass Moon, the newest school, is often favored by Westerners. Founded in 1927 by Sofu Teshigahara, Sogetsu takes the most liberties with tradition, capitalizing on the relatively recent arrival of Western flowers and foliage in Japan and adapting the art to Western settings. "There are some rules, but no arbitrary dogmas, and those rules are always flexible," explains the present master, Hiroshi Teshigahara.

Ikebana as a worldwide art form took impetus from the creation of Ikebana International in Tokyo in 1952. Ellen Gordon Allen (1897-1972), the wife of a U.S. general commanding troops in Korea, founded the international association when she lived in Japan to link masters, teachers and students around the world.

A free-form arrangement of eucalyptus branch and poppies seems to skim along the ferroconcrete wall in the Sato home. The creation is suspended by fishing line; the poppies stand in a small water container.

On the couch, the *kasuri* textiles — collectors' items — are the work of a leading Okinawan weaver Sachiko Aragaki, who used a type of ramie called *choma*. The Marcel Breuer table holds a square dish by Shōji Hamada, the dean of twentieth-century Japanese artists-potters, and a bowl by his friend for over 55 years, the British potter Bernard Leach.

▲ The Sogetsu School prizes unlikely containers. The crucial component in this wisteria and pussy willow arrangement is the brass Japanese hot water bottle, circa 1988. Colette Flipo bought it for its rippled surface to rescue her husband who was substituting as a washboard player in a Tokyo jazz group. Its acquisition launched two avocations for René Flipo: performing jazz regularly and collecting washboards from around the world. A dowry box for obi serves as end table. The portrait of Confucius is a rubbing made years ago at Longmen Caves, China.

▲ Dogwood and sweet pea in an antique bamboo basket share a niche with a roof ornament and an antique Chinese dish. The ornament is a family souvenir of their demolished Tokyo residence, as is the plywood cabinet, made shortly after the war by Antonin Raymond, a pioneer in the development of modern Japanese architecture.

Most of the arrangements in this chapter are the work of Colette Flipo, an advertising art director from South Africa, who studied *ikebana* intensively in Tokyo and became a first degree teacher in the Sogetsu School. These creations were made shortly before leaving Tokyo for Paris to launch a business featuring Japanese floral arrangements.

Collectibles

Building a collection can be satisfying in a suprising number of ways. A collector of an object that is often unappreciated talks about his passion...

"Kite flying is a way to stop time, to quiet anxieties, to eternalize the present moment." Tal Streeter, sculptor, author and professor, explains how he has come to acquire thousands of Oriental kites, probably the world's most extensive collection of this unique Asian art form. "The day I watched a construction crane swing my sculpture into place in front of New York's Metropolitan Museum, I was struck by the way the viewer's eye moved up from the base, gathered speed toward the top, and sped off into the sky, where I wanted my mind to soar. 'Why am I making sculptures?' I asked myself. I should be designing kites, and soon I went off to Japan to learn how."

The six-sided kite from Shirone in Niigata depicts Tametomo, a 12th century warrior. Legend has it that this Herculean figure in island exile tried to return his son to the mainland via a giant kite. Hand-painted on handmade paper like most Japanese kites, this piece of folk art by Toranosuke Watanabe has a prominent position in the stairway of Tal and Romig Streeter's upstate New York home. Kite spools, grouped by country, are from Japan, India, China and Korea.

▲ While writing the book *The Art of the Japanese Kite*, Mr. Streeter discovered the red, white and blue Nagasaki fighter kites by Shigeyoshi Morimoto, a famous contemporary kitemaker. They fly without a tail as all good Japanese kites must, Mr. Streeter says, but their designs are unusual for Japan since they are not hand-painted. The paper is pre-colored, cut and carefully pasted together. Finely ground glass is glued to the string so that fliers can attack each other's kites in colorful competition in the hills high above Nagasaki. Children may compete, but the contest is really one for skilled adults. Hamamatsu, three hours south of Tokyo, has a major kite-flying festival each year on May 3, 4 and 5th, as does Shirone for a week in June with six-sided fighter kites.

The kites on the right wall are from, top to bottom, India, U.S., Japan and China. The

chair is by Scandinavian designer Terje Ekstrom. On the Korean writing desk is a model of Mr. Streeter's 30-foot Olympic sculpture "Dragon Stair," now on permanent view at the National Museum for Contemporary Art in Seoul.

The pottery is by Romig Streeter who works in many different Japanese techniques. Her designs enhance specific foods.

▲ Kites with water motifs enliven the Streeter master bath. The rabbit and crane on the left wall are by Teizo Hashimoto, the last of the traditional kitemakers in Tokyo. The powerful carp, swimming upstream by Shin'ichi Muramoto, is one of the Streeters' favorite kite paintings. "It captures the vigorous and beautiful art that has graced Japan's kites for more than 300 years."

▶ It may be the Far East, but this family room wall has the homey look of the Old West. Bettie and Major General Matthew Cooper, USMC, have combined a great many antique Japanese and American tools. Among them are a Japanese clothes wringer, two kimono irons, and a "shoulder hitter" or stress reliever with the onomatopoetic name of *kata-tataki*. The open-ended basket is a winnower, a common Japanese design used to separate the chaff from rice or buckwheat.

▼ Lieutenant General J.B. and Carol Davis have a simple formula for personalizing their ever-changing homes in the U.S. Air Force (23 locations in 30 years). Since some of their residences are provided fully furnished, they can feel at home immediately by adding their collection of international folkcraft. Various Asian birdcages, part of the Davis folkcraft collection, are hung along two glass walls of their sunroom in Japan. Two of the cages shown in the photo are Japanese, while the small house on the ledge is a model of the traditional Filipino stilt dwelling.

◀ Kate Wiest uses her frequent travels around Japan to add to her collection of folkcraft toys. On the second step, the dog with the basket on his head is a charm presented to babies on their first visit to the family shrine to protect them from respiratory illness.

Near it, the egg-shaped figure is the popular Daruma, a papier-mâché doll based on the Zen patriarch, Bodhidharma. The doll comes without eyes, but the purchaser paints one eye in as he makes a wish. If the wish is fulfilled within a year, the other eye can be blackened in.

▼ "Tea sets are boring," says Amaury Saint-Gilles, author of *Earth 'n' Fire — A Guide to Contemporary Japanese Ceramics* and *"Mingei" — Japan's Enduring Folk Arts.* In his Hawaiian home/gallery, tea is always ready and the unique presentation of his one-of-a-kind cups is a reminder that in Japan it is polite to invert the cup to note the maker's mark.

Included in Mr. Saint-Gilles' collection of more than 200 cups is one by the late Nakazato Muan, who was a Living National Treasure. Such cups, a popular collectible which can sometimes be purchased fairly reasonably, appreciate over the years. The teapot is by Masatake Fukumori, whose kiln is in Marubashira near Kyoto.

Dolls of all types have always intrigued Ann Seddon, artist and author of children's books illustrated with her own handmade dolls. Mrs. Seddon says that all of these richly brocaded figures, with the exception of the padded dolls on the right, were purchased inexpensively at the outdoor markets. Most are from Hina doll sets, the collections of 15 different regal dolls traditionally displayed on Girls Day, March 3. The padded dolls are called Big Sister Dolls, *ane-sama ningyō*, and are made from kimono remnants. These particular dolls are more than 100 years old and were found at a Tokyo antique shop.

▶ Antiques become practical desk organizers for a children's book author and illustrator in Tokyo. Porcelain containers for chopsticks hold brushes; the box is an 80-year-old *suzuri-bako* for calligraphy or *sumi* supplies.

▼ Chintz and lace set the stage for a changing display of saké cup stands (*hai dai*). This collectible exemplifies on a small scale many of the qualities for which Japanese porcelain is prized — delicacy, artistry and superb craftsmanship.

◄ Since Kate and Don Wiest favor folk art, their stay in Tokyo has launched a collection of *kanban*, antique shop signs which often display ingenious imagery. The Pinocchio-like character has pickles for sale. The foot marks a store for *tabi*, special split-toed socks for Japanese sandals. The sign with gold lettering represents a fish shop, and a business in Nikko displays the product itself – a length of bamboo.

▼ With an interplay of texture, a 150-year-old Scottish pine cabinet displays Renée Kubiak's collection of antique soba cups which are further evidence of Japan's pride in creating handsome everyday objects. The cups are usually cobalt blue and white and tend to come in two sizes.

The draped silk is a prize *haori*, perhaps older than the hutch.

▲ Vintage soba cups are paired with one of John Adair's large collection of the 19th century fireman's coats, *hikeshi-hanten*. Now extremely rare on the world market, these indigo-dyed cotton coats are strengthened by Japanese quilting called *sashiko*. The padded coat was sometimes doused with water to protect the wearer from flames and falling beams. This one is hung inside out to reveal a scene depicting the 12th century rivalry between Yoritomo Minamoto, Japan's first shogun, and his younger brother Yoshitsune. Mr. Adair, owner of the Tokyo antique shop Kurofune, varies the coats on display. Firemen's hoods made in the same way are also valuable collectibles.

▲ Another rare quilted fireman's coat has a commanding position in the Adair living room. The tattooed warrior from the battle on the Gojo bridge is stitched, not painted. Beneath it is a Sendai bridal chest on wheels, designed to be moved easily to the groom's family home. Almost 150 years old, it bears the auspicious hardware of cranes and turtles, double symbols of longevity.

Mr. Adair has renovated the old Tokyo house to accommodate his 6'4" height by raising all the door lintels almost a foot and removing some interior walls. This 15-mat *tatami* room is illuminated with track lights for the art and with paper lanterns for atmosphere.

Focus on Display

Once an acquisition is made, lasting pleasure comes from being able to enjoy it on an everyday basis. Graceful positioning is key, especially when adding period pieces to Western settings. The varied photographs in this chapter share a common theme in the creative display of Japanese objects.

▶ At right, a Buddha almost 1,000 years old (from the Fujiwara regency 857-1185) is teamed with Windsor chairs, an 1800's American blanket chest acquired at a Massachusetts auction, and a silkscreen by British artist Richard Long, pasted to the wall.

▼ A collection of Buddhas has been adroitly combined with American antiques and contemporary art by a young Japanese couple who studied in the U.S.

The tiny figure below, portraying Buddha at the moment of birth, is highlighted by the folded cloth and the lacquered wood. These are called *dai*, intermediary bases often used in the Orient to make a transition between table and object. The statue is wood, Kamakura period (1185-1333), and stands on a tea ceremony cloth given to the owner by her grandmother. The figure's arm is raised asking heaven and earth to witness his arrival and proclaim his Buddhahood. An English inkstand, an American measuring beaker used as a vase, and an American 1830's drop-leaf table complete the harmony.

HEAVIER   SLOWER   SHORTER
LIGHTER   FASTER   LONGER

A FOUR DAY WALK IN ENGLAND
PICKING A STONE UP EACH DAY AND CARRYING IT.
A FOUR DAY WALK IN WALES
SETTING DOWN ONE OF THE STONES EACH DAY.

1982

▲ *Top:* A statue of a Buddhist priest, also from the Heian period (794-1185), rests on a Japanese desk. The flat black tray is a *suzuri*, an inkstone for *sumi* (ink) drawings. The end of an inkstick is rubbed against it in water to make a solution of the desired density. The trays are collectors' items in themselves, with the best made from Kyushu slate.
Below: A Korean bronze Buddha more than 500 years old has been placed on three *dai:* a silk cloth, an Edo period (1603-1868) carved base, and a richly grained board.

▲ In Kenji Tsuchisawa's Tokyo studio, a 150-year-old statue of Fujin, the god of wind, stands guard over Edo period lacquerware from Wajima in the north of Ishikawa Prefecture, one of Japan's prime centers for lacquer. The boxes were designed for food, cosmetics and paper (left to right). Completing the group are an equally old woodblock print of a kabuki actor and a portable lantern.

► George Suyama recalls with a smile the couple who came to see his collection of Japanese antiques. After a little while in the house, his visitors said, "Where are they?" Antiques were all around, but so deftly positioned that the rooms still looked extremely contemporary.

Various pieces of folk art, including antique porcelain, lacquered circular saké flasks and an heirloom basket are gracefully grouped on top of a high antique chest in the Suyama home. The arrangement also disguises two stereo speakers.

▼ Inspired by the lofts and exposed beams of his ancestral Japan, Mr. Suyama designed a ledge in his entryway to display other favorite pieces. A row of storage boxes for lanterns and candles occupies the same position it held in traditional farmhouses. Its decoration repeats a family crest.

◀ Japan's craftsmen achieve intricate textile patterns with sturdy paper stencils for *katazome* (paste-resist dyeing). These hand-cut designs, now collectors' items, had a large influence on European decorative art in the early 1900's. Barbara Kehoe has turned a dyers' stencil into a lampshade for a Meiji period jug in her home. The bronze mirror is from the same era, circa 1870. The framed forms are for making Japanese sweets.

▼ John Rogers' Long Island entry announces his design theme with a combination of fine antiques and a little theatrical staging. The screen was originally a department store prop for merchandise display. Now it unites temple candlesticks, document boxes, a picnic box and 19th century stirrups mounted on the wall.

Strategic night lighting dramatizes imposing
Asian art in one of New York's landmark
buildings which was renovated by architect
Sam Takeuchi, known for his design work at
the Metropolitan Museum of Art and the
Japan Society in New York.

The 17th century armor for a mounted
archer is an intricate combination of iron,
leather, lacquer, silk, wood and gold leaf. On
the mantel is an early Edo figure of Shōtoku
Taishi, the 7th century prince who was
devoted to the spread of Buddhism in Japan.
The silk painting is 18th century Korean,
probably a god of war. On the coffee table is
a 14th century statue of one of Buddha's
guardians.

▶ Renée Kubiak softens mini-blinds in her bedroom with a narrow side panel and a padded valance with self-tiebacks. The paper fans are the type used in traditional Japanese kitchens to fan the fire.

▼ A white-washed Asian basket dictates more Oriental touches. Mrs. Kubiak uses the lamp on an antique pine table with a woven obi and Chinese porcelain. The obi cords that unify the color scheme came from an outdoor flea market.

▲ A finely lacquered rice serving bowl becomes a central object in Renée and Dan Kubiak's elegant living room. Its atypical shape seems to be modeled after the container used for a Japanese shell game.

◀ Martine Zingg's small powder room reflects the talents of designers Renée Kubiak and Lisbeth Beise. Inspired by their client's antique, brocade-robed dolls, they swathed the room in the same delicate shades, using three commercial Japanese wallpapers to create a *tsutsugami* effect with torn edges rather than straight cuts. The mauve color between the edges is paint. An acrylic shelf allows the dolls to appear to float on air.

133

▶ "Screens with a golden background must be lit indirectly," Leighton Longhi explains, "otherwise the gold turns flat." To display his changing collection of museum quality screens in his Manhattan apartment, Mr. Longhi has designed special lighting and a platform. Light from recessed tracks in the ceiling bounces off the marble floor. Other lights concealed behind the ceiling molding play off the ceiling. The platform brings the art to eye-level, since screens were designed to be viewed while sitting on the floor. The modern Kyoto lanterns are added for atmosphere when the Longhis entertain.

On the right wall, the 19th century Japanese scroll will be the subject of a future UNICEF Christmas card. The modern cypress cat on the late Ming table is by Satoshi Yabuuchi. Presiding over the gallery is a 13th century wood carving of the Amida Buddha, the Buddha of Compassion.

▼ Seemingly contemporary, this early 17th century screen, part of the pair shown at right, has special significance for the Western world. It depicts corn and pumpkins which were unknown in Japan until they were brought by the Portuguese after the Spanish forays into the New World. The screen is from the Rimpa School, a school which shows no trace of the Chinese influence found in other Japanese periods.

◀ Gioia and Mitchell Brock's mountain home displays an ancient Japanese construction technique. Small stones serve as foundations for columns that never seem to shift or settle through centuries of earthquakes. In Japan, these small stones are set in a bed of rock and gravel sometimes two feet deep.

Architectural Elements

Of all the design fields affected by the Western world's "discovery" of Japan just 150 years ago, the field of architecture evidenced the most immediate reaction. By 1900 there were numerous examples in the West of Japanese style and Japanese-inspired homes. Eventually, international modern architecture derived key concepts from Japan as leading architects in Europe and America followed the country's lead in creating open, flexible space tied to the outdoors.

While the term "Japanese architecture" summons diverse images...ornate temples, rustic teahouses, swept-wing castles, serenely bare interiors..., constant themes emerge.

The most fundamental is the choice of wood as building material. Prized for centuries for its strength, texture, variety and color, wood is

considered most beautiful in its natural state and is rarely painted or made to look like another material.

The second essential classic characteristic is the dominant roof which often accounts for half the height of the exterior elevation. "A Japanese building is a roof," Arthur Drexler wrote in 1966 in *The Architecture of Japan*. "When the Japanese speak of the beauty of a building, they think at once of the proportions, the curvature, the sculptural modeling, and the texture of its roof." In feudal villages, a

▶ The Japanese style roof of a Long Island beach house overhangs the house by nine feet, shading both the interior and deck from the summer sun. John Wisner, a home furnishings designer and longtime admirer of Japanese aesthetics, was his own architect for Far Horizons which he named after his line of furniture.

mammoth roof was a status symbol. The length of the ridgepole, the horizontal timber at the top of the roof, dictated the social position of the occupant, and his taxes were levied according to its length. In the Edo period, a family's standing was revealed by the number of ornaments on the ridgepole which were always placed in uneven numbers.

The roof extended several feet over the walls, protecting the house from frequent driving rains. The deep eaves also shut out the high summer sun, yet admitted the low rays of winter.

The building's framework was fitted together without nails, a sort of structural cage to support the roof.

▲ The flaring and gabled roof that characterizes many buildings in Japan was the inspiration for Grey Lodge, an 18-room summer home built at the turn of the century in New York's Catskills. Its owner, Alexander Tison, taught law in Tokyo in the 1890's and, on his return to the U.S., became one of the first presidents of the Japan Society. (Photos of garden are on pages 64 and 65.)

▶ Nobuko and Kazumi Shimazaki added a touch of their native Japan to their New Jersey home a few years ago. The teahouse, created for small dinner parties, was constructed by a Japanese builder who used American pine, redwood, cedar, oak and cherry. Mylar replaces the traditional paper in the shōji.

This post and beam system made all walls non-load bearing, an effective device in a country that is rocked by frequent earthquakes. Some walls were fixed while others were not, so the side of the building could be opened to the outdoors. The movable interior partitions, *fusuma*, were lacquered frames, covered with heavy opaque paper often painted with designs.

Buildings were planned by means of fixed proportions. For example, the distance between the posts became a measure for determining the size of rooms or height of walls, assuring an overall harmony. Since homes were meant to last literally for centuries, these set proportions

◀ Rustic timbers frame the plaster walls of Alexander Tison's century-old teahouse, whose round moon window, *tsuki-mado*, is a teahouse tradition. Circular openings were strategically placed to direct sunlight to different parts of the teahouse.

allowed ready alterations as families' needs changed. In the 14th century, carpenters began to record sets of design proportions and handed them down within their own families as secret texts. By the 18th century, design books became widely circulated and eventually, the size of the *tatami*, the straw floor covering laid in mats roughly 3'x6', became the design module, determining all other proportions in the building.

The single most important feature within a traditional room is the *tokonoma*, the alcove for the appreciation of art objects, which usually consisted of a scroll and a floral arrangement. The items were changed according to the seasons. Since the Japanese are the only major civilization never to have developed furniture, the practice of sitting on the floor dictated a raised floor for warmth.

▼ Interior designer John Rogers was drawn to the round teahouse window to set off a small look-out porch on the corner of his new Southampton home. Cedar shingles and siding were combined with mahogany windows from Germany.

▼ A moon window becomes an interior design feature in a Tokyo department store display. The asymmetrical bamboo supports are also classic Japanese, since windows were often intersected by one of the bamboo wall laths to express oneness with nature.

Triple *shōji* panels — plastic sheets sandwiched between two layers of handmade Japanese paper (*washi*) — make a Fifth Avenue apartment 10 degrees warmer in winter and 10 degrees cooler in summer. "My client asked me for sensitive use of space, contour and light," Sam Takeuchi explains. Mr. Takeuchi, an architect who bridges two worlds with degrees from universities in Japan and the U.S., says "The Occidental way is to box things in, to conceal them. The Japanese expose structural parts and translate them into the scene."

Straight grain Douglas fir provides a display alcove for the rare 18th century Chinese ancestor paintings which rest on an entertainment unit. Equipment and speakers are concealed behind fabric sliders. A Shaker table and 19th century Chinese chairs echo the simple lines of the window grille housing heating and cooling units. The 800-year-old sculpture is of Kannon, the bodhisattva of mercy. The bound wheat on the table is by DuPres, Paris.

▲ A long, marble hallway in the same Manhattan apartment is made more inviting with the addition of *shōji* screens. Mr. Takeuchi concealed a small service entrance with *shōji* and then created the illusion of a wider entry by extending them along the empty wall. The "panes" are Mylar, more durable and less expensive in the U.S. than Japanese handmade paper.

A 17th century Buddha of the Ayuthya School, Thailand, marks the main entrance.

Love of nature is an essential part of the Japanese psyche and so the natural environment is usually incorporated into the design of the house. Oddly enough, old Japanese homes were designed for warm weather even though Japan's latitude spans roughly the same distance as the U.S. In winter, homeowners used to sit in bitterly cold rooms open to frozen gardens admiring the falling snow. Rooms, exterior platforms and

gardens were all situated to enjoy nature's continuing show: the plum blossoms, the cherry trees, the camellias, the fall leaves, the full moon. The appreciation of August's full moon is still an occasion for drinking saké and composing poetry.

Two building styles in particular have had a profound influence on modern architecture. The first is the rustic *minka*, the commoner's house, whose massive timber construction

▲ *Shōji* are miniaturized in Tokyo with this light fixture designed by Chikafusa Sato, who superimposed handmade paper on *shōji* style grids rather than vice versa.

▶ The innovative entrance to Eric V. and Victoria Lustbader's *tatami* room has an antique obi mounted in the *shōji*. Backed with plywood, a length of obi has been used on both sides of the sliding door. (See page 58 for a view of the room.)

145

seems to defy logic, since exposed beams rest on slender posts. "The *minka* was a prototype of the qualities prized by modern architecture: simplicity, clarity, lack of ornamentation and distinctive structure and design," wrote Teiji Itoh in *Traditional Domestic Architecture of Japan*.

The *minka* in turn inspired the teahouse, the miniscule garden sanctuary extolling simplicity, poverty and humility, where aristocracy retreated to concentrate on the transiency of the world. One of its minor features, the round window, left its mark even beyond the architectural world. A circular window frames a detail of a scene, turning the view itself into a small

picture. Japanese artists, consequently, saw pictorial themes in their immediate surroundings and translated them into round compositions on their canvases, making a picture within a picture. The circular format within a rectangle

▶ *Yuki-mi shōji* slide up to allow floor-seated residents to see snow settling on the garden. In the renovated pre-war Tokyo home of John Adair, the *shōji* combine readily with a 1700 Queen Anne tallboy, a George II corner chair and an antique Japanese saddle pad used as a throw rug.

▼ The snow-viewing principle has been reversed by the Lustbaders, who find their tree tops in all seasons more interesting than the lower portion of the view — cars in the driveway. Miya Shōji, Manhattan, executed Mrs. Lustbader's design.

became widely popular in Japan and eventually influenced European painters as well.

Aware of all these components, many private homeowners who admire Japanese style continue to borrow elements from its architectural tradition and use them to advantage in their own homes.

▼ Laurie and John Fairman, owners of Honeychurch Antiques, Seattle, transformed a room with a vaulted ceiling into one reminiscent of village houses in Japan, where John grew up. The master bedroom, executed by craftsman Steve Dowling, has concealed storage space. The back of the headboard is a storage chest; antique doors from the interior of a traditional house hide a wall of closets. The woodblock print is by Okino Hashimoto.

◄ Antique cypress doors, possibly from a small temple, have been hinged to form a screen. They bear the flowering paulownia crest of the Tokugawa Shogunate and the 16-petal chrysanthemum, the symbol of the Imperial family.

The end table at right is a bamboo "suitcase" recently relacquered. Travelers used them for clothing; merchants, for their wares.

The zelkova coffee table is an accountant's desk of Meiji vintage from Shiga Prefecture, once the location of many large trading companies.

The wall hanging is a reproduction of a wedding bed quilt cover (*futonji*) that has been handmade with new stencils from old designs. These *futonji* are available at Kurochiku Co., Kyoto.

▼ A feudal skyline carved in wood finds an original resting place in California above a reading alcove. The carving is a *ranma*, the wood transom that filled the gap between the low interior walls and the ceiling of a traditional house. Designer Lequita Vance-Watkins of Carmel found two antique *ranma* in a California antique store and used them both in her client's "Japonesque" home. The other, shown at right, decorates a high ledge

in much the same spirit as in the traditional house. Above the chest, a *shōji* screen has been turned into a decorative wall hanging.

Ranma were designed to provide light and let air circulate, and ranged from simple geometric grilles to elaborate scenes. Their creative motifs influenced the applied arts in Japan, providing inspiration for dyers' stencils, lacquerwork and textiles.

Four homes, four viewpoints

1. A transplanted, renovated *minka* hugs a hilltop overlooking the sea in Kamakura, an hour from Tokyo.
2. In the hills of Los Gatos, California, a conventional contemporary house has been deftly modified, capturing the spirit of Japanese aesthetics.

3. A Japanese style house nestles in an isolated valley of the Catskills, providing an unusual vacation retreat for a large New York family.

4. Inspired by Japanese design, a summer home stands in marked contrast to its neighbors on eastern Long Island, but in concert with the terrain and climate.

Each of these four houses is home to an individual with an overriding commitment to Japanese design. Their stories appear on the pages that follow.

YOSHIHIRO TAKISHITA

With a law degree from Waseda University in his back pocket, Yoshihiro Takishita decided to take 18 months off and hitchhike around the world. Visiting European and American museums in 1967, he focused for the first time on the beauty of Japanese art and returned home to become a specialist in antiques and the restoration of a massive form of "folk art," the *minka* or Japanese rural house.

Mr. Takishita buys the centuries-old structures, disassembles them and rebuilds them anywhere in the world for his customers. Over the years, he has rebuilt 21 houses, transporting some as far away as Hawaii and Argentina. The task amounts to assembling a child's construction set with as many as 5,000 giant pieces to be notched or tied together. Mr. Takishita carefully repositions the tongue-in-groove beams and implants 20th century comforts: central heating, air conditioning, insulation, modern kitchens and baths. At the same time, he rigorously maintains the integrity of the original structure, and he has been widely acclaimed for architectural preservation.

He and his wife Reiko make their home and gallery in a 250-year-old *minka* in Kamakura which he moved from the mountains of his native Gifu, a region famous for its carpenters. "Having lived in a minka as a child, I grew up to admire its polished dark beams, its marvelous proportions, its spaciousness and its feeling of history," he says. Two other restored *minka* on the same hill provide additional gallery space. Mr. Takishita considers his work "a never ending study and pleasure" and says that his current inventory of 14 dismantled *minka* waiting in storage are "like my children, waiting to be born. When I sell one, it is like my daughter going away to be married."

▼ Rough-hewn zelkova beams, positioned to capitalize on their natural curve, show the notched construction that makes disassembly possible. In an earthquake, the construction rocks gently. With the posts and beams supporting the building, the walls bear none of the weight. The *minka* home serves as a gallery for the business that Mr. Takishita heads, House of Antiques, which specializes in screens, porcelains, baskets and chests, some of which can be seen in the photos.

◀ Mr. Takishita added floors and landings to the two-story house to create four levels and unique display space. At the far left, a Shinto goddess in a 15th century camphor wood carving commands attention on a landing shared with a 100-year-old writing desk and a 200-year-old plate.

▼ An unconventional display window, cut high in the wall, reminds visitors there is more to see upstairs.

◀ Almost 400 years old, a *daimyō's* statue recalls feudal Japan, when the regional lords represented military power, administrative and judicial authority, and the pinnacle of the arts of their time. The statue rests on a Chinese 18th century rosewood stand.

▶ The *gasshō* roof is now several layers: stucco on reed supports braced by ancient cedar crosspieces, a layer of insulation, and shingles instead of thatch. Fresh rice straw cords bind the original timbers. The steep roof, which originated in snow country, derives its name from the word *gasshō*, which means the position of hands in prayer, palms together.

▲ The hardware on the antique documents chest indicates its Sado Island origin. A *zabuton* (pillow) covered with *asa* fabric (hemp) for summer is pulled up to the 18th century Chinese table. The contemporary chair is from Takayama.

▶ Using an old technique, Mr. Takishita has stripped the bark from a branch and turned it into an authentic looking stair rail for his restored home. The loft serves as Mrs. Takishita's music room and affords a view of Mt. Fuji, which is considered a good omen.

◀ Capitalizing on the faceted roof similar to Japanese village houses, Chadine renders her theme at the front door with artfully placed stone steps. The loose black pebbles are spread over existing tiles. The *shōji* fixture that sheds light on this "important intermediate space" is made with 1/8" fiberglass.

CHADINE FLOOD GONG

The road twists and turns through a lush canyon. Houses dot the hillsides, half-concealed by trees. Then at the end of a long driveway…a surprise. A matte black house sits in the sunshine, nestled between a hill and a running creek. Its lines are blurred by groves of chalky green eucalyptus and brilliant green bamboo.

"Sometimes the smallest thing can make a world of difference," explains its owner, the diminutive interior designer who in California goes simply by the name Chadine. Her home is a composite of carefully considered details that she has slowly added, and at times subtracted, to create a cohesive Japanese feeling. Many are inexpensive and exemplify Japanese resourcefulness in using natural materials.

Chadine taught at a Tokyo university in the 1960's. Those years intensified her interest in Japanese aesthetics which began as a student in her native Thailand and continued after as a professor of Asian Studies in California.

"I have always been drawn to Japanese design and for years have submerged myself in it. When I design interiors or courtyard gardens, part of what I do is based on study, the other part is the result of feeling things in the Japanese way."

Ten years ago, Chadine and her physician husband, Dr. Hayman Gong, bought a nondescript house that seemed to be all brown, inside and out. The first thing Chadine did was remove some of the deck railings to suggest a Japanese *engawa* (veranda). Then, in spite of everyone's protests, she painted the exterior charcoal. Small windows gave way to glass walls to invite nature in. Her *shōji* screen supplier, Wren Okasaki, marvels at her ability to suggest more with less, citing the living room where Chadine gives the illusion of a much larger window by strategic placement of panels. "All her design solutions," Wren says, "appear so simple when they are done, but these understatements involve a great deal of thought."

▶ Chadine's interior renovation began in the dining room when she installed her first black *shōji* for insulation against the summer heat. It accords with the stone table and the screen, mounted unconventionally. The Zen circle stands for anything flawless and perfect, a graphic reference to the all-embracing virtue of Buddha. The plates are antique Imari; the chopsticks, silver.

▲ Under the sheltering roof, a Japanese fence accentuates the front door and insures privacy on the bedroom balcony beyond. It is made of twigs and bamboo in an untraditional curve. The stone basin, used in Japan for a purifying ritual at shrines and teahouses, is to remind the owners and guests to discard anxieties before entering.

▶ Chadine changed the style of the window and door casings, extending the lintels slightly. The *shōji* window treatment and free-standing screen are by Design Shōji of Redwood City. A Japanese garden lantern sits by the fire. The porcelain *hibachi* (brazier) with the plant is on a wooden *hibachi* used as an end table.

▼ A few well chosen pieces of wood and bamboo plus *shōji* totally transform an existing bath. Chadine mounted a hand-cut textile stencil over a sheet of blue paper and framed it as a work of art. (Other views of the house are on pages 50 and 68.)

GIOIA BROCK

As a child in a small town in New York's Catskill Mountains, Gioia Brock played at a neighboring house filled with treasures from Japan. (See the Tison estate, page 138.) The house was surrounded by unique Japanese gardens where the children invented games amid stone lanterns, bridges and a teahouse, imagining the hills and rivers of Japan.

This first exposure to Japanese beauty led to others over the years, including the study of moss which the Japanese cultivate so patiently. One day someone lent her a book on the Katsura Imperial Villa in Kyoto, the quintessential Japanese retreat with its gardens of moss and rock, and she knew she had found inspiration for a future home. Decades later, when it came time to build on the family estate, her husband, Mitchell, suggested a site with a view of the sunset, a feature her parents' house in the valley lacked. Mrs. Brock remembered riding her horse to a hill to watch the sunset and knew it would be ideal for her Japanese dream house.

An American architect, A. Perry Morgan, drew up plans and construction began in 1976. Cherry trees on the property were felled, milled and kiln-dried to provide interior flooring and paneling. They also provided the house's name "Yamazakura So" — Mountain-Cherry Villa.

"There are still more things we would like to do," Mrs. Brock explains. But the finishing touches will have to wait, since Mitchell and Gioia Brock now make their home, as luck would have it, in Tokyo, where Mr. Brock's business took him two years ago.

The house, however, continues to draw the Brocks' four children and to emanate the calm that marks all traditional Japanese interiors.

▶ Two unassuming rocks make invulnerable front steps; their appearance can only improve with age. A moss and fern garden line the path. The macramé cord is a downspout, made by one of the Brock children. It is a variation on the Japanese chain that turns rain spilloff into an appreciation of nature. (See page 68.)

▲ On the approach, only a narrow wing of the house is visible. Entering the front door, the visitor has no idea of the size or plan of the four-bedroom house. As in a Japanese garden or in many elaborate buildings in Japan, its features reveal themselves one by one. "It looks like a small cottage from the road," Mrs. Brock explains. "We like the Japanese element of mystery, the idea of surprise."

◀ A carved *ranma*, the delicate transom that fills the space between the top of the wall and the ceiling in the traditional house, spans the entrance to the dining room. Craftsman Shigeru Kobayashi imported the contemporary *ranma* from the town of Inami in Toyama Prefecture, but used local wood for framing details.

▼ In order to create a sense of anticipation for what lies ahead, Japanese architects do not always design rooms adjoining each other. The rooms are linked by hallways, which sometimes serve chiefly as an aesthetic device. In the Brock home, this passageway with flooring of local black cherry, leads to the living room.

Like musical variations, Douglas fir has been worked into multiple designs to echo the faceted ceilings of the steeply pitched village roofs. The *shōji* windows overlook a swimming pool in a natural setting. The ceiling *shōji* conceal light fixtures.

◀ Traditionally, large sliding paper doors carried a painting or design. As classical rooms became more Western, sliding doors were replaced by hinged doors, sometimes decorated. Gioia and Mitchell Brock wallpapered a conventional door for this modified style. The checkerboard paper on the closet sliders, and on pages 164 and 165, is a copy of the wallpaper of the teahouse at the Katsura Imperial Villa in Kyoto. Its atypical pattern and bright color were designed to be seen across the lake in the Villa. The Nakashima bench is a free-form interpretation of a Shaker piece.

◀ Japanese craftsmanship sings in every room. The octagonal pass-through window is a perfect circle on the kitchen side. The cupboard's wooden doors slide effortlessly in any weather without metal fittings.

The dining table, made of rare Indian laurel, and the cherry wood chairs are by the late George Nakashima, who was considered the elder statesman of the American crafts movement. Born in the U.S. and trained as an architect, he became interested in Japanese carpentry while working in Tokyo in 1937. He honed his furniture-making skills in the 1940's in an Idaho detention camp for Japanese Americans by studying with a fellow internee trained as a carpenter in Japan.

Mr. Nakashima often turned flaws in wood to artistic advantage. "The 'uniqueness' imparted by the imperfections," he wrote, "makes these pieces appealing." Part of his mission was to "give some trees a fitting and noble purpose, helping them live again." The butterfly joint in the foreground was Mr. Nakashima's signature method for holding wood together.

JOHN WISNER

"I remember exactly what triggered my interest. It was a book on Japanese architecture that someone gave me as a teenager. Ever since then I have been drawn to Japanese aesthetics."

John B. Wisner's Eastern penchant has manifested itself continuously through his long and distinguished career in home furnishings design. His sentimental favorite work is an Oriental line of furniture, Far Horizons, that he designed for Ficks Reed which sold steadily for many years. That is why, Mr. Wisner says with a twinkle, he named his home on the shore of Long Island "Far Horizons."

The house rides like a ship in a salt water meadow where masses of reeds sway with the breeze. Wraparound decks — one with a swimming pool — and several Japanese gardens afford a continuous link with the outdoors.

Constructed in 1961, the house derives its basic plan from the Japanese modular system. The walls are composed of industrial fiberglass panels, three feet wide, with a core of polyurethane foam. Their linen-like finish requires no maintenance either on the interior or exterior. Mr. Wisner designed the house utilizing local building materials, but brought finishing details from Japan and the West Coast.

▲ Looking very much like a Japanese *minka* with its weathered cypress frame, Far Horizons is topped with a traditional roof ornament, whose original function was to prevent leakage at the end of the ridge.

◀ Classic bronze finials, which preserve the posts from the effects of excessive weathering, accent the front steps.

▲ The timeless design theme is carried throughout the house. The dressing cabinet in the Japanese bathroom bears a contemporary artist's adaptation of a Meiji era print by Yoshiiku of a woman's bathhouse.

▲ The quiet beauty of a weathered, bamboo fence mounted in a cypress frame marks the approach to a smaller building on the Wisner property. The treatment is distinctly Japanese: more fence isn't needed since the mind completes the picture. (Other views of the garden are on pages 60, 61 and 63.)

▶ As the setting sun turns John Wisner's *tatami* room golden, dinner guests can be transported East. When night falls, the silk globes diffuse candlelight on the 18th century six-panel screen and antique tableware. The blue and white wallpaper is a reproduction inspired by the Katsura Imperial Villa in Kyoto. To the right is an antique brazier, *hibachi*, made from a tree trunk. The basket in the foreground with the unusual lid is a Japanese fish trap.

◀ An antique *ranma*, carved with the "Three Friends of Winter" — pine, bamboo and plum — serves a new architectural function. Mr. Wisner found a matched pair in a San Francisco antique store and used them with backlighting to delineate niches on both sides of the fireplace. The Schumacher fabric on the sectional, inspired by a brocade obi, is Mr. Wisner's design, as are the small tables created for Ficks Reed. The lacquered pieces are antique, stacking food boxes used outdoors for flower-viewing parties and indoors on festive occasions.

▼ The flexible exterior wall of old Japanese houses allowed replacement in the summer of the *shōji* panels with fine screens of split bamboo. The screens make ideal doors for closet ventilation in the waterfront home.

Historical Periods

Jōmon (Neolithic)
ca. 10,000–
ca. 200 B.C.

Yayoi
ca. 200 B.C.–
ca. 200 A.D.

Kofun (Tumulus)
200 A.D.–593

Asuka
593–710

Nara
710–794

Heian
794–1185

Kamakura
1185–1333

Muromachi
(Ashikaga)
1333–1573

Azuchi Momoyama
1573–1603

Ēdo (Tokugawa)
1603–1868

Meiji
1868–1912

Taisho
1912–1926

Showa
1926–1989

Heisei
1989–

Resources

Page 13: Sink cabinet designed by James Porter of Bay Contract Interiors, 2793 16th Street, San Francisco, CA 94103, Tel: (415) 863-8043, and Audrey Owens, 569 Buena Vista Terrace, San Francisco, CA 94117, Tel: (415) 626-6731.

Page 32: Stand for *ranma* sofa table designed by Barbara Wilson, Robert Brian Co., Galleria/Design Center, 101 Henry Adams, Space 136, San Francisco, CA 94103.
Tel: (415) 621-2273.

Pages 37, 50, 101, 158, 159: Shōji screens by Design Shōji, 841 Kaynyne, Unit B, Redwood City, CA 94063.
Tel: (415) 363-0898. Sales representatives in several states.

Page 56: Shōji screens by Henry Nakata, Aspen Ten, 140 E. Jackson, San Jose, CA Tel: (408) 923-4902. Designer — Lequita Vance-Watkins, AdVance Design, 25553 Flanders Drive, Carmel, CA 93923. Tel: (408) 624-5068.

Pages 76, 98: Comforters, pillows, place mats, napkin rings by Naomi Iwasaki Hoff, 5-12-3 Shiroganedai, Minato-ku, Tokyo 108. By appointment only. Tel: 444-9263.

Page 107: Ikebana International, C.P.O. Box 1262, Tokyo 101-91, Japan. Tel: (03) 293-8188, Fax: (03) 294-2272. For information on *ikebana* classes in the U.S., call (415) 567-1011 (Ikenobo Society), (212) 564-0841 (Ohara Center), and (301) 321-0811 (Sogetsu U.S.A.).

Page 111: Colette Flipo teaches *ikebana* at 130 rue de Tocqueville, Paris 75017. By appointment only.
Tel: 47-66-78-48.

Page 129: Lampshade from dyers' stencil by Richard James, 874 Hamilton Drive, Pleasant Hill, CA 94523.
Tel: (415) 939-1587.

Page 143: Architect for apartment renovation — Sam Takeuchi, 38-25 Woodside Avenue, Woodside, NY 11377.
Tel: (212) 935-4711.

Page 149: Design concept for Japanese bedroom by Doug Rasar, 12440 North East 24th, Bellevue, WA 98005. Craftsman — Steve Dowling, 6729 Sycamore North West, Seattle, WA 98117.

Page 160: Architect for Brock house — A. Perry Morgan Jr., Holt & Morgan Associates P.A., 350 Alexander Street, Princeton, NJ 08540. Tel: (609) 924-1358. Master craftsman for interiors — Shigeru Kobayashi, Tonee Crafts Corporation, 108 Wooster Street, New York, NY 10012. Tel: 966-4213.

BAMBOO

The American Bamboo Society, comprising 900 members in 35 countries, each year publishes a source list for bamboo plants. Their current list numbers 119 species and specifies 26 dealers in various parts of the U.S., many of whom ship worldwide. To obtain a free copy, send a self-addressed, stamped envelope with your request to The American Bamboo Society, P.O. Box 640, Springville, CA 93265.

Bamboo may also be ordered from Bamboo & Rattan Inc., 470 Oberlin Avenue South, Lakewood, NJ 08701.
Tel: (201) 370-0220.

Specialized Shops

Antiques and folkcraft can be acquired in a variety of ways in Japan, depending upon inclination and timetable. Department stores are a useful source, especially in the field of folkcraft when demonstrations and special exhibits are held. Outdoor markets are another interesting experience. Vendors from all parts of Japan assemble on a regular basis on the grounds of certain shrines, providing a rich selection and a wide range of prices. The schedule for these markets appears on the following pages. The most obvious source — established antique shops — are the most convenient in terms of daily availability and reliable quality. In addition, they have sales people who speak English and will provide receipts documenting origins of pieces. There are many excellent shops, but the following have been especially helpful in the preparation of this book.

For antiques:

House of Antiques, 5-15-5 Kajiwara, Kamakura. By appointment only. Tel. (0467) 43-1441. Fax (0467) 45-8245.

Fuso Antiques, 1-20-2, Kamata, Ohta-ku, Tokyo 144. Tel. (03) 730-6530 or 442-1945. 10 to 6. Closed Saturdays and Sundays.

Kikori Antique Gallery, 1-9-1, Hibarigaoka, Hoya-shi, Tokyo 202. Tel. (0424) 21-7373. 10 to 6. Retail and wholesale.

Kurochiku Co. Ltd., 34 Takenokaido-cho, Takehana, Yamashina-ku, Kyoto. Tel. (075) 501-8491. Fax (075) 501-8493.

Kurofune, 7-7-4 Roppongi, Minato-ku, Tokyo 106. Tel. 479-1552. 10 to 6. Closed Sundays, holidays.

Magatani Co. Ltd., 5-10-13 Toranomon, Minato-ku, Tokyo 105. Tel. 433-6321. 10 to 6. Closed Sundays and holidays.

Morita, 5-12-2 Minami Aoyama, Minato-ku, Tokyo 107. Tel. 407-4466. Weekdays 10 to 7, Sundays and holidays 12 to 6.

Nakamura Antiques, 2-24-9 Nishi-azabu, Minato-ku, Tokyo 106. Tel. 486-0636. 10:30 to 6:30. Closed Tuesdays. Retail and wholesale.

Okura Oriental Art, 3-3-14 Azabudai, Minato-ku, Tokyo 106. Tel. 585-5309. 10 to 6. Closed Mondays.

Osugi Shoten, Gokomachi Sanjo Sagaru, Nakagyo-ku, Kyoto 604. Tel. 231-7554.

For folkcraft:

Bingoya, 10-6 Wakamatsu-cho, Shinjuku-ku, Tokyo 162. Tel. 202-8778. 10 to 7. Closed Mondays.

Oriental Bazaar, 3-9-13 Jingumae, Shibuya-ku, Tokyo 150. Tel. 400-3933. 9:30 to 6:30. Closed Thursdays. Also carries antiques.

Prefecture Showrooms, Daimaru Department Store and Kokusai Kanko Building, next to Tokyo Station. Yaesu North Exit. Many regional handicrafts displayed by prefecture on the 8th and 9th floors of Daimaru and in approximately 30 showrooms in the adjacent Kokusai Kanko Building, floors 2,3 & 4. Hours 10-5:30. Sat. 10-12:30. Kokusai Tel. 215-1181. Closed Sundays. Daimaru closed Wednesdays. Tel. 212-8011.

Washikobo, 1-8-10 Nishi-Azabu, Minato-ku, Tokyo 106. Tel. 405-1841. 10 to 6. Closed Sundays, holidays.

Regional Craft Centers

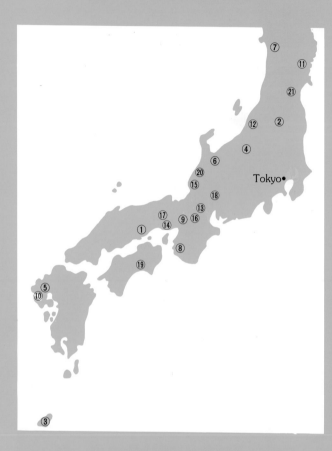

Tokyo•

The following centers, administered by local municipal governments or artisan associations, display examples of local traditional crafts. Most offer the items for sale, and many schedule demonstrations or videos of craftsmen at work. Since this is the first time this list has been made available in English, most of the centers are not accustomed to receiving English-speaking guests. It is advisable to have someone who speaks Japanese make arrangements. All the centers are closed during the New Year's holidays and most charge a nominal admission fee.

This information has been supplied by the Japan Traditional Craft Center in Tokyo, where changing exhibitions of the country's crafts offer continuing shopping opportunities. This non-profit center was established by the Ministry of International Trade and Industry to publicize crafts and distribute information. Their address: Plaza 246 Building, 2nd floor, 3-1-1 Minami Aoyama, Minato-ku, Tokyo 107. Tel. 403-2460. Open 10-6. Closed Thursdays.

1. Bizen-yaki Traditional Craft Center
1657-2, Inbe, Bizen City, Okayama Pref. 705
Pottery exhibition, lectures. Closed Tuesdays.
Tel. (0869) 64-1001
From Okayama Station, 45 min. on the JR Ako Line to Inbe Station. Exhibit is on 2nd and 3rd floors in Inbe Station Building.

2. Fukushima-ken Traditional Craft Center
1-7-3, O-machi, Aizu-Wakamatsu-shi, Fukushima Pref. 965
Display and sale of lacquerware and pottery. Closed Sundays and holidays. Tel. (0242) 24-5757
From Koriyma Station, 1 hour 20 min. on Express JR Banetsu-Saisen Line to Aizu-Wakamatsu Station, then 15-min. walk.

3. Homba Oshima Tsumugi Traditional C. Ctr.
15-1, Minato-machi, Naze City, Kagoshima Pref. 894
Pongee textile exhibition, information, videos.
Closed Sundays, holidays and Saturday afternoons.
Tel. (0997) 52-3411
From Kagoshima Airport, 20 min. flight to Amami Oshima Airport, then 1 hr. by express bus to Naze-shi.

4. Iiyama-shi Traditional Craft Center
1436-1, Oaza Iiyama, Iiyama City,
Nagano Pref. 389-22
Display and sale of family altars, handmade paper, lacquerware, pongee, furniture, lathe wooden crafts, and handmade cutlery.
Closed Mondays. Tel. (0269) 62-4019
From Nagano Station, 50 min. on JR Iiyama Line to Iiyama Station, then 10-min. walk.

5. Imari Arita-yaki Traditional Craft Center
222, Okawachi-cho Hei, Imari City, Saga Pref. 848
Exhibition of Imari ware, Arita ware, Ko-Imari, Ko-Nabeshima ware.
Lectures. Closed Mondays. Tel. (0955) 22-6333
From Hakata Station, 2 hours on JR Chikuhi Line to Imari Station, then 16 min. by bus to Okawachi-yama.

6. Inami Chokoku Traditional Craft Center
700-111, Inami-machi Inami, Higashi Tonami-gun, Toyama Pref. 932-02
Display and sale of wood carvings.
Closed Mondays. Tel. (0763) 82-5158
From Maibara Station 2 1/2 hours on Express JR Hokuriku Honsen Line to Takaoka Station. Then 50 min. by bus to Inami-machi, plus 10-min. walk.

7. Kakunodate-machi Birch Traditional C. Ctr.
10-1, Kakunodate-machi Omote-machi Shimo-cho, Semboku-gun, Akita Pref. 014-03
Display and sale of birch crafts, Shiraiwa pottery, lacquerware, maple wood crafts, armor, folkcrafts.
Closed Thursdays from Nov. to March.
Tel. (01875) 4-1700
From Morioka Station, 1 hour on express to Kakunodate Station, then 15-min. walk.

8. Kishu Shikki Traditional Craft Center

222, Funoo, Kainan City, Wakayama Pref. 642
Lacquerware exhibit and information.
Closed Aug. 14-16. Tel. (07348) 2-0322
From Shin Osaka Station, 5 minutes to Umeda Station on
JR Tokaido Honsen Line. Then 1 hour on Express JR Kisei
Honsen Line to Kainan Station, plus 5 min. by taxi.

9. Kyoto-shi Traditional Craft Center

9-2, Okazaki Seishoji-cho, Sakyo-ku, Kyoto City,
Kyoto Pref. 606
Exhibition of textiles (nishijin-ori, yuzen, shibori) braid,
pottery, furniture, family altars, lacquerware, cutlery, fans,
dolls, metalwork, bamboo crafts and more. Movies, videos,
demonstration.
Closed Mondays. Tel. (075) 761-3421. From Kyoto
Station, 40 min. by bus to Bijutsukan Mae.

10. Mikawachi-yaki Traditional Craft Center

343, Mikawachi Hon-machi, Sasebo City,
Nagasaki Pref. 859-31
Display and sale of pottery, raku-yaki, kiln tour.
Tel. (0956) 30-8080. From Nagasaki Airport, 1 hour 20
min. by bus to Tagonoura, then 15 min. by bus to Dento
Sangyo Kaikan.

11. Mizusawa-shi Traditional Craft Center

1-109, Hada-cho Ekimae, Mizusawa City,
Iwate Pref. 023-01
Ironware exhibition, videos.
Closed Mondays. Tel. (0197) 23-3333
From Ueno Station, 2 hours 48 min. by JR Tohoku
Shinkansen to Mizusawa Esashi Station.

12. Ojiya-shi Traditional Craft Center

1-8-25, Jonai, Ojiya-shi, Niigata Pref. 947
Display and sale of textiles — crepe and pongee — woven
by Living National Treasures. Also family altars and other
local products. Weaving demonstrations.
Closed Mondays. Tel. (02588) 3-2329. From Nagaoka
Station, 40 min. by bus to Ojiya Hon-cho, 3-chome.

13. Omi Jofu Traditional Craft Center

13-7, Oaza Echigawa, Echigawa-cho, Echi-gun,
Shiga Pref. 529-13
Display and sale of ramie textiles. Occasional weaving
classes. Closed Sundays, holidays, 2nd Saturdays, and
Saturday afternoons. Tel. (07494) 2-3246
From Maibara Station, 22 min. on JR Tokaido Honsen
Line to Notogawa Station, then 20 min. by Omi bus to
Echigawa Yakuba Mae.

14. Ono-shi Traditional Craft Center

806-1, Oji-cho, Ono City, Hyogo Pref. 675-13
Exhibition of abacus, pottery, metalwork, wood crafts, fish
hooks. Demonstrations.
Closed holidays. Tel. (07946) 2-3121
From Shin-Kobe Station, 10 min. by bus or taxi to
Sannomiya Station, then 1 hr. 10 min. by Kobe Dentetsu
Line to Ono Station, plus 10-20 min. walk.

15. Sabae-shi Echizen Shikki Traditional C. Ctr.

37-6-1, Nishi-bukuro-cho, Sabae City, Fukui Pref. 916-12
Display and sale of lacquerware. Occasional videos.
Closed Aug. 13-16. Tel. (0778) 65-0030
From Maibara Station, 1 hr. on JR Hokuriku Honsen Line to
Sabae Station, then 25 min. by bus from Shimizu-cho to
Nishi-bukuro-guchi.

16. Shigaraki Traditional Craft Center

1142, Oaza Nagano, Shigaraki-cho, Koga-gun,
Shiga Pref. 529-18
Exhibition of pottery.
Closed Thursdays. Tel. (07488) 2-2345
From Kyoto Station, 16 min. by Tokaido Honsen Line to
Ishiyama Station, then 1 hr by bus to
Dento Sangyo Kaikan Mae.

17. Tamba Tachikui-yaki Traditional Craft Center

3, Kami-Tachikuibo-no-gaki, Konda-cho, Taki-gun,
Hyogo Pref. 669-21
Display and sale of pottery.
Closed Aug. 13-15. Tel. (07959) 7-2034
From Shin-Osaka Station, 5 min. on JR Tokaido Line to
Umeda Station, then 1 hr. 20 min. on JR Fukuchi-yama Line
to Aino Station, then 15 min. by taxi.

18. Toki-shi Mino-yaki Traditional Craft Center

1429-8, Izumi-cho Kujiri, Toki City, Gifu Pref. 509-51
Display and sale of pottery.
Closed Mondays and day after national holidays.
Tel. (0572) 55-5527
From Nagoya Station, 2 1/2 hrs. by Express JR Hokuriku
Line to Takaoka Station, then 50 min. by bus to Inami-machi,
plus 10-min. walk.

19. Tosa Washi Traditional Craft Center

110-1, Ino-cho Saiwai-cho, Agawa-gun,
Kochi Pref. 781-21
Display and sale of handmade paper and folkcrafts.
Demonstrations, videos.
Closed Mondays. Tel. (0888) 93-0886. From Kochi Airport,
30 min. by bus to Kochi Station, then 20 min. by Dosansen
Line to Ino Station, plus 10-min. walk.

20. Yamanaka Shikki Traditional Craft Center

268-2, Yamanaka-machi Tsukatani-machi 1,
Enuma-gun, Ishikawa Pref. 922-01
Display and sale of lacquerware.
Tel. (07617) 8-0305
From Maibara Station, 1 1/2 hours by Express JR Hokuriku
Honsen Line to Kaga Onsen Station, then 20 min. by taxi.

21. Zao-machi Traditional Craft Center

36-135, Aza Shinchi Nishi Urayama, Tokatta Onsen,
Zao-cho, Katta-gun, Miyagi Pref. 989-09
Display and sale of kokeshi dolls of Tohoku area and
wooden toys.
Tel. (02243) 4-2385
From Shiraishi Zao Station, 40 min. by bus to Zao Tokatta
Onsen, then 5-min. walk.

Antique Markets in Japan

The following list of periodic antique markets in Japan represents open markets where vendors congregate, usually outdoors, to sell their wares. The merchandise falls into every category including genuine antiques, attic junk and intentional fakes.

The atmosphere is exhilarating with negotiation a must. The most determined shoppers arrive at opening time to compete with the antique store owners in search of the best buys.

TOKYO

Antique Market, 30 dealers
Hanae Mori Bldg., 3-6, Kita Aoyama, Minato-ku, Tokyo
3 minute walk from Omote-sando Station
(Subway Ginza Line)

Arai Yakushi Antique Fair, 80 dealers
Arai Yakushi Temple, First Sunday of each month
10 minute walk from Arai Yakushi Station (Seibu Line)

Boro-ichi Antique Market, 50 dealers
Boro-ichi Street, December 15-16 and January 15-16
5 minute walk from Setagaya Station
(Tokyu Setagaya Line)

Hanazono Shrine Antique Market, 80 dealers
Hanazono Shrine, Second and Third Sundays
5 minute walk from Shinjuku San-chome Station
(Subway Marunouchi Line)

Heiwajima Antique Market, 200 dealers
Heiwajima-Tokyo Ryutsu Center Bldg. at Ryutsu Center Station on Tokyo Monorail Line from JR. Hamamatsucho Station. Three consecutive days, four times a year in a modern exhibition hall (with restaurant facilities). For exact dates, call 950-0871. It is the most important single market in Japan.

Ikebukuro Antique Market, 30 dealers
Ikebukuro Sunshine Bldg., Third Saturdays and Sundays
10 minute walk from JR Ikebukuro Station

Nogizaka Antique Market, 50 dealers
Nogi Shrine, Second Sunday of each month
Nogizaka Station (Subway Chiyoda Line)

Ramla Antique Market
Ramla Bldg., First Saturday of each month
3 minute walk from JR Iidabashi Station

Roppongi Antique Fair, 30 dealers
Roppongi Roi Bldg., Fourth Thursdays and Fridays
10 minute walk from Roppongi Station
(Subway Hibiya Line)

Shofuda-kai Antique Market
Tokyo Bijutsu Club, Early July and Early December (two days each, call 431-6060 for exact dates).
15 minute walk from Onarimon Station
(Subway Mita Line)

Togo No Mori Antique Market, 70-90 dealers
Togo Shrine, First and Fourth Sunday of each month
10 minute walk from JR Harajuku Station

Tokyo Antique Hall
2-9, Kanda Surugadai, Chiyoda-ku, Tokyo
5 minute walk from JR Ochanomizu Station

TOKYO SUBURBS

Kawagoe Antique Market, 50 dealers
Narita-fudo Temple, The 28th of each month
15 minute walk from Hon-Kawagoe Station
(Seibu Line)
Saiunji Temple, The 14th of each month
10 minute walk from Kawagoe Station (Seibu Line)

Sagami Antique Market, 10 dealers
Atsugi Shrine, First Saturday of each month
5 minute walk from Honatsugi Station (Odakyu Line)

Shonan Antique Market, 20 dealers
Yugyoji Temple, First Sunday of each month
20 minute walk from JR Fujisawa Station

Takahata Fudo Market, 15 dealers
Takahata Fudo Temple, Third Sunday of each month
5 minute walk from Takahata Fudo Station (Keio Line)

Urawa Antique Market, 30 dealers
Sakuraso Street, Fourth Saturday of each month
3 minute walk from JR Urawa Station

NAGANO

Karuizawa Antique Market
Kyu-Karuizawa Public Hall, August 1-31,
15 minute walk from JR Karuizawa Station

NAGOYA AREA

Henshoin Antique Market, 15 dealers
Henshoin Temple, Every 21st on Lunar Calendar
5 minute walk from Chiryu Station (Meitetsu Line)

Osu Kannon Antique Market, 30 dealers
Osu Kannon Temple, The 18th and 28th of
each month
Near Osu Kannonmae Station (Subway Tsurumai Line)

KYOTO

Kobo Antique Market, 50 dealers
Toji Temple, First Sundays, The 21st of each month
5 minute walk from Toji Station (Kintetsu Line)

Tenjin Antique Market, 100 dealers
Kitano Tenmangu Shrine, The 25th of each month
30 minutes by bus from JR Kyoto Station

OSAKA

Daishi Antique Market, 200 dealers
Osaka Shitennoji Temple, The 21st of each month
5 minute walk from Shitennojimae Station
(Subway Tanimachi Line)

Hatsu Tatsu Mairl Market, 25 dealers
Sumiyoshi Taisha Shrine, first Dragon Day of
each month
5 minute walk from Toriimae Station (Nankai
Hankai Line)

Koshindo Antique Market, 30 dealers
Koshindo Temple, Every Sunday
5 minute walk from Shitennoji-mae Station
(Subway Tanimachi Line)

Ohatsu Tenjin Antique Market, 12 dealers
Ohatsu Tenjin Shrine, First Friday of each month
5 minute walk from Umeda Station (Hanshin Line)

Sankaku Koen Antique Market
Sankaku Park, Every Sunday
5 minute walk from Dobutsuen-mae Station
(Subway Midosuji Line)

KOBE

Kobe Antique Market, 30 dealers
Sumadera Temple, First Sunday of each month
5 min. walk from Sumadera Station
(Sanyo Dentetsu Line)

HIROSHIMA AREA

Cancan Bazar (Kurashiki City), 30 dealers
Ivy Square, Consecutive national holidays
in May and Oct.
15 minute walk from JR Kurashiki Station

Sumiyoshi Antique Market (Fukuyama City)·
10 dealers
Sumiyoshi Square, Fourth Sunday of each month
15 minute walk from JR Fukuyama Station

These schedules are subject to change.

Shopping Sources in The United States and Canada

The following list is a sampling of retail establishments dealing in objects from Japan. Goods range from antiques of museum quality to structural items like *shōji* screens. Some museums are also listed both for inspiration and for the shopping possibilities offered by their gift stores. The museums are marked with an * for ready reference.

ARIZONA

Orient East
6204 N. Scottsdale Road
(Lincoln Village Shops)
Scottsdale 85253
(602) 948-0489
Furnishings, artifacts

CALIFORNIA

Abacus
1012 Alma Street
Menlo Park 94025
(415) 323-5893
Antiques and folkcraft

Asakichi
1730 Geary Boulevard
San Francisco 94115
(415) 921-2147
Furniture, porcelain,
Japanese accessories

* **Asian Art Museum
of San Francisco**
Avery Brundage Collection
Golden Gate Park
San Francisco 94118-4598
(415) 668-8921

Roger Barber
114 Pine Street
San Anselmo 94960
(415) 457-6844
Antiques

Elaine Barchan Interiors
2261 Highland Oaks Drive
Arcadia 91006
By appointment
Antique textiles and obi

Blue Horizons
205 Florida Street
San Francisco 94103
(415) 626-1602
Shōji manufacturer specializing
in custom color matches

Robert Brian Co.
Galleria/Design Center
101 Henry Adams, Space 136
San Francisco 94103
(415) 621-2273
Wide selection of antiques,
tansu and folkcraft.
Principally wholesale.

Bunka-Do
340 East First Street
Los Angeles 90012
(213) 625-8673
Folkcraft, ceramics

Arlene Cox Textiles
750 Adella Avenue
Coronado 92118
(619) 435-3054
By appointment
Antique *mingei* textiles

The Crane and Turtle
2550 California Street
San Francisco 94115
(415) 567-7383
Wide collection of fine & folk
art, antique and contemporary

Den Japanese Art Salon
444 South Flower Street
Los Angeles 90017
(213) 489-1508
Changing exhibition of traditional
crafts presented by Japan Center
for Traditional Crafts, Tokyo. Items
can be ordered.

Design Shōji
841 Kaynyne, Unit B
Redwood City 94063
(415) 363-0898
Sales reps in several states
Custom-made *shōji*

Elica's Paper
1801 Fourth Street
Berkeley 94710
(415) 845-9530
Washi—wide selection of
handmade paper

Dodi Fromson
P.O. Box 49808
Los Angeles 90049
(213) 451-1110
By appointment
Antiques, textiles,
bronzes, metalwork,
lacquerware

Fumiki Fine Arts
2001 Union St.
San Francisco 94123
(415) 922-0573
Obi, porcelain, *tansu*, *netsuke*

The Gallery
27 Malaga Cove Plaza
Palos Verdes Estates 90274
(213) 375-2212
Antiques

Genji
501 York St.
San Francisco 94110
(415) 255-2215
and
1731 Buchanan Street
San Francisco 94115
(415) 931-1616
Wide selection of chests,
folk art and kimono

Gump's
250 Post Street
San Francisco 94108
(415) 982-1616
800-652-1662 dialing within Ca.
800-227-3135 from out of state
and
9560 Wilshire Boulevard
Beverly Hills 92000
(213) 278-3200
Wide collection of antiques,
furniture and art objects

Hayashi Oriental Antiques
1894 Union Street
San Francisco 94123

House of Crispo
425 Cannery Row
Monterrey 93940
(408) 373-8467
Porcelain, *netsuke*,
Oriental art

Habitat
158 East Tahquitz-McCallum Way
Palm Springs 92262
(619) 325-4042
Antique porcelain

International Trading Co.
950 E. 11th Street
Los Angeles 90012
(213) 629-5554
Noren, *yukata*

Japan Gallery
2624 Wilshire Boulevard
Santa Monica 90403
(213) 453-6406
Netsuke, *tansu*, baskets, kimono

Japan Interiors
1840 Fulton Avenue
Sacramento 95825
(916) 486-1251
Shōji, tatami, gifts

The Japan Trading Co.
1762 Buchanan Street
San Francisco 94115
(415) 929-0989
Shōji, tatami, fusuma

Japonesque
50 Post Street
Crocker Center Galleria, 54
San Francisco 94104
(415) 398-8577
Wide selection of antique and
contemporary home furnishings

Kasuri Dye-Works
1959 Shattuck Avenue
Berkeley 94704
(415) 841-4509
Kasuri, silk, *yukata* fabric by
the yard, wooden folkcrafts.
Mail order video available

Kura Antiques
1849 Union Street
San Francisco 94123
(415) 921-4117
Antiques and arts

Kuromatsu
722 Bay Street
San Francisco 94109
(415) 474-4027
Antiques, *mingei*

Larchmont Japanese Antiques
115 N. Larchmont Boulevard
Los Angeles 90004
(213) 467-0430
Antiques

∗ **Lowie Museum of Anthropology**
University of California
Campus at Berkeley
(415) 643-7648, 642-3681

∗ **Los Angeles County
Museum of Art**
Japanese Pavillion
5905 Wilshire Boulevard
Los Angeles 90036
Shops: (213) 857-6146, 6520

Marukai Corp.
15725 S. Vermont Avenue
Gardena 90247
(213) 538-4025
Kimono

Marukyo U.S.A.
New Otani Hotel Arcade
110 S. Los Angeles Street
Los Angeles 90012
(213) 628-4369
Kimono, obi, fabrics

Marumasu
336 East Second Street
Los Angeles 90012
(213) 628-5198
Kimono

McMullen's Japanese Antiques
146 N. Robertson Boulevard
Los Angeles 90048
(213) 652-9492
and
1615 Stanford St.
Santa Monica 90404
(213) 828-7479
(213) 828-3023
Tansu, folk art, lacquerware,
kimono, porcelain, ceramics,
obi, screens

Mikado (J.C. Trading, Inc.)
1737 Post Street
San Francisco 94115
(415) 922-9450
Kimono, *futon,* interior decorations

∗ **Mingei International Museum
of World Folk Art**
4405 La Jolla Village Drive, Bldg. 1-7
San Diego 92122
(619) 453-5300

Nichi Bei Bussan
1715 Buchanan Mall
San Francisco 94115
(415) 346-2117
and
140 Jackson Street
San Jose 95112
(408) 294-8048
Kimono, folk art, *noren,*
yukata by the yard

Shige Nishiguchi
Japan Center
1730 Geary Boulevard
San Francisco 94100
(415) 824-0857
New and antique kimono

Oriental Arts
1206 Orange Avenue
Coronado 92118
(619) 435-5451
Lacquerware, porcelain

Oriental Corner
280 Main Street
Los Altos 94022
(415) 941-3207
Antiques, *netsuke,* lacquerware,
porcelain

Oriental Porcelain Gallery
2702 Hyde Street
San Francisco 94109
(415) 776-5969
19th century porcelain

Oriental Treasure Box
Olde Cracker Factory
Antique Shopping Center
448 W. Market Street
San Diego 92101
(619) 233-3831
Tansu, kimono, obi, lacquerware, folk
art, porcelain, textiles, *hibachi,* dolls

Orientations
34 Maiden Lane
San Francisco 94108
(415) 981-3972
and
189 North Robertson Blvd.
Beverly Hills 90212
(213) 659-7431
Porcelain, baskets, *tansu,* screens

∗ **Pacific Asia Museum**
46 N. Los Robles Avenue
Pasadena 91101
(818) 449-2742

Sakura Horikiri
Tozai Plaza
15480 S. Western Av.
Gardena, 90249
(213) 323-1821
Washi

∗ **San Francisco Art Institute**
800 Chestnut
San Francisco 94100
(415) 771-7020
Washi (gift shop)

Soko Hardware
1698 Post Street
San Francisco 94115
(415) 931-5510
Kites (upstairs), porcelain,
chopstick rests (downstairs)

Soko Interiors
1672 Post Street
San Francisco 94115
(415) 922-4155
Folkcraft, furniture,
lacquerware, porcelain

Takahashi Oriental Decor
235 15th St.
San Francisco 94103
(415) 552-5511
Wide selection of *tansu,* textiles,
screens, furnishings, folkcraft,
shōji, ceramics, obi bronzes

Takahashi Trading Corp.
200 Rhode Island St.
San Francisco 94103
(415) 431-8300
Screens, *shōji,* doors, *ranma,*
scrolls, paintings

Tansu Collections
Box 1396
Menlo Park 94025
(415) 323-6272
By appointment
Tansu, textiles, *mingei*, customized
furniture

Tokyo Gift Shop
Lincoln and Ocean Avenue
Carmel 93921
(408) 624-3646
Antique porcelain, screens,
furniture

Townhouse Living
1825 Post Street
San Francisco 94115
(415) 568-1417
Kimono, obi, folkcraft, furniture

Warren Imports
1910 South Coast Highway
Laguna Beach 92652
(714) 494-0150
and
73-199 El Paseo Avenue
Palm Desert 92660
(619) 340-9410
Very large selection including
Tansu, porcelain, screens,
scrolls, obi, lacquerware,
bronzes, *netsuke* and
candlesticks

The Zentner Collection
5757 Landregan Street
Emeryville 94608
(415) 653-5181
Very large selection of
antiques, especially *tansu*
and *mingei*

COLORADO

Blue Willow Gallery
1437 Market Street
Denver 80202
(303) 572-3297
Antiques

CONNECTICUT

**Graynook Antiques and
Interiors**
72 Park Avenue
Bridgeport 06604
(203) 334-3621
By appointment
Wedding kimono, Imari

The Kura
310 Rockrimmon Road
Stamford 06903
(203) 329-1778
By appointment
Hibachi, *tansu*, lamps, obi,
baskets, screens

Midori
7 Campbell Drive
Stamford 06903
(203) 322-3205
By appointment
Wide variety of antiques & folk
craft including dolls, Imari, *tansu*

Tradewinds
1749 House
Goshen 06756
(203) 491-2141
Antiques and artifacts

Vallin Galleries
516 Danbury Road (Rte. 7)
Wilton 06897
(203) 762-7441
Fine porcelain, *tansu*, *hibachi*,
stone lanterns, art

DELAWARE

Rita Connolly
516 Beechtree Lane
Gateway Townhouses
Hockessin 19707
(302) 658-5486
(302) 239-9096
By appointment
Dolls, antique obi

DISTRICT OF COLUMBIA

Arise Gallery
6295 Willow St., N.W.
Washington, D.C. 20012
(202) 291-0770
Kimono, obi, *tansu*, *hibachi*,
screens, *ranma*, dolls, baskets,
porcelain, prints

Asian Art Center
2709 Woodley Pl., N.W.
Washington, D.C. 20008
(202) 234-3333
Porcelain, lacquerware, screens

∗ **Freer Gallery of Art**
Smithsonian Institution
Jefferson Dr. at 12th St., S.W.
Washington, D.C. 20560
(202) 357-1300 museum
357-1429 museum shop

Ginza
1721 Connecticut Ave., N.W.
Washington, D.C. 20008
(202) 331-7991
Antique kimono, folk art, porcelain,
crafts, *futon*

Harding-Giannini Antiques
Tenjin-san, Inc.
1083 Wisconsin Avenue, N.W.
Washington, D.C. 20007
(202) 333-5999
Ceramics, textiles, *tansu*, folkcraft

Shogun Gallery
1083 Wisconsin Avenue, N.W.
Washington, D.C. 20007
(202) 965-5454
Woodblock prints, sword guards,
dolls, *netsuke*

∗ **The Textile Museum**
2320 S Street, N.W.
Washington, D.C. 20008
(202 667-0441

FLORIDA

**Carol Croll
Asian Accents**
4238 45th St. S.
St. Petersburg, 33711
Washi eggs, kimono, *washi* jewelry

Ehrenkranz & Epstein Inc.
P.O. Box 430852
South Miami 33243
(305) 751-1719, 661-0944
Netsuke, inro, ojime

Galleries
234 Worth Avenue
Palm Beach 33480
(407) 655-6114
Fine art

Harper Galleries/Bijutsu, Inc.
333 Worth Avenue
Palm Beach, 33480
(407) 655-8490
Traditional furnishings,
art and accessories

∗ **Morikami Museum and
Japanese Gardens**
4000 Morikami Park Road
Delray Beach 33446
(407) 495-0233

Palm Beach Interiors Inc.
309 Peruvian Avenue
Palm Beach 33480
(407) 832-3461
Antique porcelain, paintings,
furniture

Vilda B. de Porro
311 & 209 Worth Avenue
Palm Beach 33480
(407) 655-3147
Hibachi

GEORGIA

Art Gallery Colony Square
1197 Peachtree Street, N.E.
Atlanta 30361
(404) 261-1233
Arts and crafts

**J.H. Elliott Appraisal and
Antique Company**
537 Peachtree Street, N.E.
Atlanta 30308
(404) 872-8233
Antiques

**Sahara Japanese Architectural
Woodworks, Inc.**
1716 Defoor Place N.W.
Atlanta 30318
(404) 355-1976
Home construction, teahouses,
wood craft

HAWAII

Bushido
936 Maunakea Street
Honolulu 96817
(808) 536-5693
Fax: (808) 521-1994
Ceramics, kimono, obi, swords

Garakuta-do
444 Hobron Lane
Honolulu 96815
(808) 955-2099
and
938 Maunakea Street
Honolulu 96817
(808) 536-5786
Tansu, screens, Imari, *mingei*,
textiles

＊Honolulu Academy of Arts
900 South Beretania Street
Honolulu 96814
(808) 538-3693

Mills Gallery
701 Bishop Street
Honolulu 96815
(808) 536-3527
Antiques, folkcraft,
interior design

Amaury Saint-Gilles
P.O. Box 13
Ninole, Hawaii 96773
Tel. and Fax (808) 962-6884
By appointment only
Contemporary fine art

ILLINOIS

Aiko's Art Materials
3347 N-Clark St.
Chicago 60657
(312) 404-5600
Washi, contemporary Japanese
prints

Saito Incorporated
Suite 410,
840 North Michigan Avenue
Chicago 60611
(312) 642-4366
By appointment
Porcelain, bronzes, sculpture,
lacquerware

J. Toguri Mercantile Co.
851 West Belmont Avenue
Chicago 60657
(312) 929-3500
Home furnishings, lacquerware,
kimono

KENTUCKY

Boones Antiques
4996 Old Versailles Road
Lexington 40504
(606) 254-5335
Porcelain, furniture

＊Headley-Whitney Museum
4435 Old Franklin Pike
Lexington 40500
(606) 255-6653
Porcelain

Wakefield-Scearce
525 Washington Street
Shelbyville 40065
(502) 633-4382
Masks, porcelain

LOUISIANA

**Imperial Dragon
Oriental Imports**
4100 General de Gaulle Drive
New Orleans 70100
(504) 393-2832
Fans, screens, kimono

＊New Orleans Museum of Art
City Park
New Orleans 70100
(504) 488-2631
Large collection of Asian art

**Oriental Art and Antiques of
Diane Genre**
233 Royal Street
New Orleans 70130
(504) 525-7270
Antiques, screens, furniture,
prints, textiles and lacquerware

MAINE

Barbara Forlano
P.O. Box 462
Chases Pond Road
York 03909
(207) 363-7009
19th century needlework,
some porcelain

Ross Levett Antiques
Tenants Harbor 04843
(207) 372-8407
Antiques

Sign of the Owl
Coastal Route 1
Northport
Mailing address: P.O. Box 85 RR2
Lincolnville 04849
(207) 338-4669
Changing collection including
kimono, obi, *netsuke* and prints

MARYLAND

Knight-Flight
P.O. Box 2518
Gaithersburg 20886
(301) 921-0386
Ceramics, furniture, textiles,
silver, bronzes, woodblock prints,
religious items, interior decoration
and appraisal services

MASSACHUSETTS

Alberts-Langdon, Inc.
126 Charles Street
Boston 02114
(617) 523-5954
Furniture, paintings, porcelain

Bernheimer's Antique Arts
52-C Brattle Street
Cambridge 02138
(617) 547-1117
Ceramics, prints, paintings,
netsuke, mingei

＊Children's Museum
300 Congress Street
Boston 02210
(617) 426-6500

Dynasty Gallery
377 Route 20
Sudbury 01776
(508) 443-5573
and
1033 Massachusetts Ave.
Cambridge 02138
(617) 864-8449
Furniture, lamps, *hibachi, tansu*,
obi, porcelain, artwork

Eastern Accent
237 Newbury Street
Boston 02116
(617) 266-9707
Contemporary, handcrafted
designs for dining and the home.
Catalog available

Robert C. Eldred Co., Inc.
1483 Route 6A
East Dennis 02641
(508) 385-3116
Wide selection of antiques,
arts and accessories

＊Isabella Stewart Gardner Museum
280 The Fenway
Boston 02115
(617) 566-1401

Kiku Sui Gallery
101 Charles Street
Boston 02114
(617) 227-4288
Antique and modern Japanese
prints

Kobo Kamiya
1280 Centre Street
Bay 2, Newton 02159
(617) 964-5665
Washi and paper crafts

Samuel L. Lowe, Jr. Antiques
80 Charles Street
Boston 02114
(617) 742-0845
Antiques, porcelain, prints

＊Museum of Fine Arts, Boston
465 Huntington Avenue
Boston 02115
(617) 267-9300

**＊George Walter Vincent
Smith Art Museum**
222 State Street
Springfield 01103
(413) 733-4214

＊Peabody Museum of Salem
161 Essex
Salem 01970
(617) 745-9500
Folkcraft

Sanpho America
189 State Street
Boston 02109
(617) 720-5370
Folkcraft, kimono, furniture

Vilunya Folk Art
Vilunya Diskin
Charles Square 5 Bennett Street
Cambridge 02138
(617) 661-5753
Folkcraft, kimono, *hanten*, obi, *haori*,
lacquered boxes

Weiner's Antique Shop
22 Beacon Street (cor. Park)
Boston 02108
(617) 227-2894
Antiques

MICHIGAN

D and J Bittker Gallery Ltd.
536 N. Woodward
Birmingham 48011
(313) 258-1670
Antiques

Dulany's Gallery
4000 Quarton Road
Bloomfield Hills 48013
(313) 645-2233 or 645-7475
Antiques

The Lotus Gallery
119 East Liberty
Ann Arbor 48104
(313) 665-6322
Antiques

MINNESOTA

Asian Fine Arts
825 Second Avenue South
Minneapolis 55402
(612) 333-4740
Antique and contemporary
artwork

Sharen Chappell
P.O. Box 9091
North St. Paul 55109
(612) 777-8910
Netsuke, lacquerware

MISSISSIPPI

East West Antiques
400 Cherokee Drive
McComb 39648
(601) 684-4638
Large selection of antique silk obi

MISSOURI

Asiatica Ltd.
205 Westport Road
Kansas City 64111
(816) 931-9111
Furniture, textiles, kimono,
obi, *mingei*

Brookside Antiques
6219 Oak Street
Kansas City 64113
(816) 444-4774
Furniture, woodblock prints,
porcelain, cloisonné

＊Nelson-Atkins Museum of Art
4525 Oak Street
Kansas City 64111
(816) 561-4000

NEW HAMPSHIRE

The Garakuta Collection
65 Bow Street
Portsmouth 03801
(603) 433-1233 or 964-9241
Antiques and contemporary
objects—*tansu*, *mingei*, textiles,
woodblock prints

NEW JERSEY

Ivory Bird
555 Bloomfield Avenue
Montclair 07000
(201) 744-5225
Imari, prints, embroidery

NEW MEXICO

Mary Hunt Kahlenberg
1571 Canyon Road
Santa Fe 87501
(505) 983-9780 by appointment
Textile arts

Little Shop
Water Street Plaza
138 West Water Street
Santa Fe 87501
(505) 984-1050
Fine art

NEW YORK

Art Asia, Inc.
1088 Madison Avenue (81st St.)
New York City 10028
(212) 249-7250
Kimono, obi, lacquerware,
porcelain, baskets, furniture

Asia Society
725 Park Avenue
New York City 10021
(212) 288-6400
keyaki stationery boxes, ironware
teapots, ceremonial teacups —
Shino ware

Azuma Gallery
50 Walker Street
New York City 10013
(212) 925-1381
Woodblock prints, ceramics,
sculpture, swords

Bonsai Designs
1862 Newbridge Road
North Bellmore 11710
(516) 785-5397
Nursery plus custom-designed
interiors and exteriors

＊Brooklyn Museum
200 Eastern Parkway
Brooklyn 11238
(718) 638-5000

Crestwood
315 Hudson Street
New York City 10013
(212) 989-2700
Toll Free: 800-344-2692
Fax: (212) 929-7532
Largest importer of Oriental
papers in U.S. Call for retail sources
in 50 states, Canada and abroad

Daikichi
Madison Street
Sag Harbor 11963
(516) 725-1533
In Manhattan by appointment:
(212) 532-2192
Wide variety of furnishings and
textiles

Design Studio of Southampton
225 Windmill Lane
Southampton 11968
(516) 283-4666
Interior design, chests and fine
home furnishings

Eastern Dreams
6 Greenridge Drive
Chappaqua 10514
(914) 666-8910
by appointment only
Porcelain, *yukata*, lacquerware,
paper and wood crafts, *ikebana*
planters, contemporary screens

Edo Antiques Ltd.
67 East 11th Street
New York City 11011
(212) 254-2508
Furniture, porcelain, art

80 Papers
510 Broome Street
New York City
(212) 431-7720
Opens at Noon Monday thru Sat.
and 1pm Sun.
Washi

Five Eggs
436 West Broadway
New York City 10012
(212) 226-1606
Antiques, kimono, ceramics,
mingei, *yukata*, *tatami*

Flying Cranes Antiques
Manhattan Art & Antique Center
1050 Second Avenue (56th St.)
New York City 10022
(212) 223-4600
Antiques—Imari, silver, cloisonné,
money chests

Gordon Foster Antiques
1322 Third Avenue (75th St.)
New York City 10021
(212) 744-4922
Mingei, baskets, *tansu*, ceramics,
porcelain

Charles R. Gracie & Sons, Inc.
979 Third Avenue
New York City 10022
(212) 753-5350
Tansu, *hibachi*, screens

Grillion Corporation
189-193 First Street
Brooklyn 11215
(718) 875-8545
Shōji

Inouye Japanese Gardens, Inc.
97 Lawrence Hill Road
Cold Spring Harbor 11743
(516) 427-9704
(718) 380-4258
Landscaping, Japanese fences,
teahouses, rock gardens

∗ **Japan House**
333 East 47th Street
New York City 10017
(212) 832-1155
Books, posters

Japanese Screen
23-37 91st Street
East Elmhurst 11369
(718) 803-2267
Shōji, *tatami*, *fusuma*, lamps

John Rogers
63 Main Street
Southamptom 11968
(516) 283-0715
Lacquerware, housewares

Jomon Gallery
550 Madison Ave. (55th St.)
New York City 10022
(212) 935-1089
Monday-Saturday 11-6
Fine traditional craftwork

Kate's Paperie
8 West 13th Street
New York City 10011
(212) 633-0570
Wide selection of *washi*

Kimono House
120 Thompson St.
New York City 10012
(212) 966-5936
Antique kimono and small items

Koto
71 West Houston Street
New York City 10012
(212) 533-8601
Kimono, lacquerware, screens,
contemporary ceramics, crafts

Leighton R. Longhi
P.O. Box 6704
New York City 10128
Fax: (212) 996-0721
Museum quality fine art

Lord & Taylor
424 Fifth Avenue
New York City 10018
(212) 391-3344
Tansu (8th floor),
antique Imari (9th floor)

∗ **Metropolitan Museum of Art**
Fifth Avenue at 82nd Street
New York City 10028
(212) 879-5500
Gift shop: *netsuke*, lacquerware,
ceramics, posters

Miya Shoji & Interiors, Inc.
109 West 17th Street
New York City 10011
(212) 243-6774
Japanese rooms. *shōji*, *fusuma*, light
fixtures, stone lanterns

Naga Antiques Ltd.
145 East 61st Street
New York City 10021
(212) 593-2788
Sculpture, ceramics, furniture,
lacquerware, screens

Orientations Gallery
Place des Antiquaires
Gallery Twenty-two
125 East 57th Street
New York City 10022
(212) 371-9006
19th century Edo and Meiji art,
cloisonné, Satsuma, metalwork,
bronzes, ivory, and wood carvings,
netsuke, lacquerware, *inro*, *ojime*

Pillow Perfections
12 Stuyvesant Street
New York City 10003
(212) 528-5183
Tatami

Ronin Gallery
605 Madison Avenue
New York City 10022
(212) 688-0188
Woodblock prints (17th through
20th century), *netsuke*, pottery,
sword guards

Sugimoto
120 East 64th Street
New York City 10021
(212) 751-0650
By appointment only
Museum quality antique art and
sculpture, antique and contemporary
ceramics, archeological pieces.

Talas
213 W. 35th Street
New York City
(212) 736-7744
Closed from 11:30–1
Mon. thru Fri.
Handmade Japanese paper

Tansuya Corporation
159 Mercer Street
New York City 10012
(212) 966-1782
Furniture, screens, lacquerware

Things Japanese
1109 Lexington Avenue, (2nd fl.)
New York City 10021
(212) 249-3591
Mingei, kimono, obi, baskets,
Imari, furniture, *netsuke*, dolls

Tokyo Arts Salon
Manhattan Art & Antique Center
1050 Second Avenue (56th St.)
New York City 10022
(212) 888-7195
Kimono, antique Imari

Tsuru Gallery
22 East 66th Street
New York City 10021
(212) 772-6422
Woodblock prints, screens, paintings

Joanne Wise
The Wise Collection
4 Morningside Circle
Bronxville 10708
(914) 961-9325
Contemporary ceramics, artwork,
sculpture

Yuzen Ltd.
318 East 6th Street
New York City 10003
(212) 473-3405
Kimono, wedding kimono, yukata,
antique and contemporary

Zen Oriental Bookstore
521 Fifth Avenue
New York City 10017
(212) 697-0840
Washi, ceramics, dolls

OHIO

Mary Baskett Gallery
1002 St. Gregory Street
Cincinnati 45202
(513) 421-0460
Ceramics, Oriental art

Ginko Tree
Dillonvale Shopping Center
4389 East Galbraith Road
Deerpark, Cincinnati
(513) 984-0553
Ceramics, porcelain

*Cleveland Museum of Art
1150 East Boulevard
Cleveland 44106
(216) 421-7340

Mitzie Verne Collection
John Carroll University
The Grasselli Library Gallery
20700 North Park Boulevard
University Heights 44118
(216) 397-4551
Mail to: 3326 Lansmere Road
Shaker Heights 44122
Contemporary & antique prints,
hand stencil dyed prints, screens,
scrolls, contemporary ceramics

OREGON

Nelson & Yoshizu Antiques
521 Southwest 11th Avenue
Portland 45770
(503) 228-4436
Antiques and art

Shibumi Trading Ltd.
P.O. Box 1-F
Eugene 97440
Outside of Oregon:
1-800-843-2565
In Oregon: (503) 683-1331
Antique kimono, obi, books, stone
lanterns, basins, wide selection of
folkcraft. Mail order catalog available.

Shogun's Gallery
206 Northwest 23rd Avenue
Portland 97210
(503) 224-0328
Mingei, tansu, textiles, porcelain

PENNSYLVANIA

Pearl of the East
Willow Grove Park
Springfield Mall
1615 Walnut Street
Philadelphia 19100
(215) 563-1563
Furnishings, porcelain,
futon bedding

Sanctuary Futon Company
217 Church Street
Philadelphia 19106
(215) 925-9460
Futon, tatami

Three Cranes Gallery
18-20 Mechanic Street
New Hope 18938
(215) 862-5626
Tansu, porcelain, textiles, prints,
shōji, tatami

RHODE ISLAND

Nortons' Oriental Gallery
415 Thames Street
Newport 02840
(401) 849-4468
Antiques

Oriental Arts Ltd.
Brickmarket Place
Newport 02840
(401) 846-0655
Antiques, reproductions, accessories
and furniture

SOUTH CAROLINA

The Red Torii
197 King Street
Charleston 29401
(803) 723-0443
Porcelain, netsuke, bronzes, cloisonné

TEXAS

Asian Arts
1980 Post Oak Boulevard
Houston 77000
(713) 629-9797
Antiques and art

*Kimball Art Museum
3333 Camp Bowie Blvd.
P.O. Box 9440
Fort Worth 76107
(817) 332-8451

East & Orient Company
2901 North Henderson
Dallas 75206
(214) 826-1191
Fax: (214) 821-8632
Porcelain, lacquerware, screens

Gump's
The Galleria, Suite 1105
13350 Dallas Parkway
Dallas 75240
(214) 392-0200
Antiques, lanterns, screens

Janet Lashbrooke
Oriental Antiques
112 Sugarberry Circle
Houston 77024
(713) 953-9144
Tansu, mingei, baskets, teapots

Loyd-Paxton, Inc.
3636 Maple Avenue
Dallas 75219
(214) 521-1521
Textiles, lacquerware, screens,
porcelain, bronzes, cloisonné

Translations
4811 Abbott
Dallas 75205
(214) 522-1115, 351-0285
By appointment
Home accessories, antique and
contemporary

WASHINGTON

Asia Gallery
1220 First Avenue
Seattle 98101
(206) 622-0516
Wide selection of antiques &
folkcraft, including textiles,
furniture, baskets, masks,
porcelain

The Crane Gallery, Inc.
1203 B Second Avenue
Seattle 98101
(206) 622-7185
Asian art

Honeychurch Antiques Ltd.
1008 James Street
Seattle 98104
(206) 622-1225
Furniture, ceramics, paintings,
woodblock prints, sculptures

Japanese Antiquities Gallery
200 East Boston Street
Seattle 98102
(206) 324-3322
Monday through Friday 9-4,
Saturday by appointment
Antique folk art, furniture,
ceramics

Kagedo
55 Spring Street
Seattle 98104
(206) 467-9077
          and
1100 Western Avenue
Seattle 98101
(206) 467-5847
Antiques and folk art

Marvel on Madison
69 Madison
Seattle 98104
(206) 624-4225
Folk crafts, ceramics, *tansu*,
lacquerware

Noh Mask
285 Bellevue Square
Bellevue 98004
(206) 455-9773
Kimono

Andy Shiga's One World Shop
4306 University Way NE
Seattle 98100
(206) 633-2400
Kimono

* **Seattle Art Museum**
14th E. & E. Prospect
Seattle 98100
(206) 625-8900
Textiles, art

Uwajimaya
6th Ave. S. and S. King St.
Seattle 98104
(206) 624-6248
Washi, shōji lamps, kimono, *noren,
ikebana* vases

CANADA

TORONTO

Dolly Beil Ltd.
986 Eglinton Avenue, W.
Toronto, Ontario M6C 2C5
(416) 781-2334
Kutani & Satsuma porcelain

Gallery Shioda
98 Avenue Road
Toronto, Ontario M5R 2H3
(416) 961-2066
Wide selection of antiques,
including kimono, *hibachi* and *tansu*

Japanese Paper Place
966 Queen Street, W.
Toronto, Ontario M6J 1G8
(416) 533-6862
Washi, including *shōji*,
stencilled paper and paper
for origami

Okame Japanese Antiques
709 Devonshire Road
Windsor, Ontario N8Y 2L9
(519) 254-4363
By appointment
Ceramics, antique kimono & obi,
baskets, scrolls, dolls, metalwork,
woodblock prints and folk art

Ozawa Canada Tea Importer
135 E. Beaver Creek Rd., Unit 7
Richmond Hill, Ontario L4B 1E2
(412) 731-5088
Tea chests

VANCOUVER

Japanese Accents Kiku
1532 Marine Drive
West Vancouver, B.C. V7V 1H8
(604) 925-2584
Tansu, chabako, mingei, textiles
and ceramics

Potter's Gallery
665 Howe Street
Vancouver, B.C. V6C 2E5
(604) 685-3919
Imari, Satsuma, Kutani

Dorian Rae Collection
3151 Granville Street
Vancouver, B.C. V6H 3K1
(604) 732-6100
          and
2033 West 4th Avenue
Vancouver
(604) 732-6100
Paintings, screens, dolls, ceramics,
hibachi

**Frankie Robinson
Oriental Gallery**
3055 Granville Street
Vancouver, B.C. V6H 3J9
(604) 734-6568
Tansu, mingei, Satsuma, *hibachi*,
screens

Bibliography

Austin, Robert; Levy, Dana; Ueda, Koichiro, *Bamboo*, Walker/Weatherhill, New York, Tokyo, 1970

Brandon, Reiko Mochinaga, *Country Textiles of Japan, The Art of Tsutsugaki*, Weatherhill, New York, 1983

Coe, Stella, *Ikebana*, The Overlook Press, Woodstock, New York, 1984

Davidson, A.K., *The Art of Zen Gardens*, J.P. Tarcher, Inc., Los Angeles, 1983

Drexler, Arthur, *The Architecture of Japan*, The Museum of Modern Art, New York, 1955

Engel, David H., *Japanese Gardens For Today*, Charles E. Tuttle, Rutland, Vermont and Tokyo, 1959

Frédéric, Louis, *Japan, Art and Civilization*, Harry N. Abrams, Inc., New York, 1969

Hauge, Victor & Takako, *Folk Traditions in Japanese Art*, Kodansha, Tokyo, New York, 1978

Heineken, Ty & Kiyoko, *Tansu*, Weatherhill, New York, Tokyo, 1981

Holborn, Mark, *The Ocean in the Sand*, Shambhala Publications, Boulder, Colorado, 1978

Ishimoto, Tatsuo & Kiyoko, *Japanese Gardens Today*, Crown Publishers, Inc., New York, 1968

Itoh, Teiji, *Space & Illusion in the Japanese Garden*, Weatherhill, New York, Tokyo, Kyoto, 1973

Itoh, Teiji, *Traditional Domestic Architecture of Japan*, Weatherhill/Heibonsha, New York, Tokyo, 1972

Iwamiya, Takeji; Yoshida, Mitsukuni; Gage, Richard L., *Forms, Textures, Images*, Weatherhill, New York, Tokyo, 1979

Kawashima, Chūji, *Minka, Traditional Houses of Rural Japan*, Kodansha International, Tokyo, New York, 1986

Kincaid, Viola W., *Japanese Garden and Floral Art*, Hearthside Press, Inc., New York, 1966

Koizumi, Kazuko, *Traditional Japanese Furniture*, Kodansha International, Tokyo, New York, 1986

Kroh, Patricia, *Japanese Flower Arrangement Notebook*, Doubleday & Co., New York, 1962

Lancaster, Clay, *The Japanese Influence in America*, Abbeville Press, New York, 1983

Lowe, John, *Japanese Crafts*, Van Nostrand Reinhold Company, New York, 1983

March-Penny, John, *Japanese Flower Arrangement*, Hamlyn Publishing Group, Ltd. Feltham, Middlesex, England 1969

Massy, Patricia, *Sketches of Japanese Crafts*, The Japan Times, Tokyo, 1980

Moes, Robert, *Mingei, Japanese Folk Art*, The Brooklyn Museum, Universe Books, New York, 1985

Munsterberg, Hugo, *Zen and Oriental Art*, Charles E. Tuttle Co., Rutland, Vermont and Tokyo, 1965

Murphy, Wendy B. and Time-Life Editors, *Japanese Gardens*, Time-Life Books, Alexandria, Virginia, 1979

Nishi, Kazuo & Hozumi, Kazuo, *What is Japanese Architecture?*, Kodansha, Tokyo, New York, 1983

Saint-Gilles, Amaury, *Mingei, Japan's Enduring Folk Arts*, Amaury Saint-Gilles, 1983

Shimizu, Yoshiaki, editor, *Japan, The Shaping of Daimyo Culture 1185-1868*, George Braziller, Inc., New York, 1988

Statler, Oliver et al., *All-Japan: The Catalogue of Everything Japanese*, Columbus Books, Kent, England, 1984

Streeter, Tal, *The Art of the Japanese Kite*, Weatherhill, New York, Tokyo, 1974

Suzuki, Hiroyuki and Banham, Reyner, *Contemporary Architecture of Japan*, Rizzoli International, New York, 1985

Wichmann, Siegfried, *Japonisme: The Japanese Influence on Western Art in the 19th and 20th Century*, Harmony Books, New York, 1981

— *Kodansha Encyclopedia of Japan*, Kodansha, Tokyo, New York, 1983

— *Plants and Gardens*, periodical published by Brooklyn Botanic Garden, Inc., Autumn 1985

Glossary

Arita: ceramics made in the Arita region in Saga Prefecture, Kyushu. Also known as Imari ware, after the port from which the ceramics were exported.

Asahi ware: Pottery made at Uji, Kyoto Prefecture, since the early 17th century. Tends to be made of a coarse, sandy clay. Kiln is still in production and is well known for its modern, computer-controlled technology.

Bizen ware: unglazed stoneware made in Okayama Prefecture from the 12th century (possibly earlier) to the present. Typical wares have a vitrified body with surfaces of glossy gold, matte orange, iridescent blue-green, or rough, charcoal-like patches, all produced by sustained, high temperature firings.

bodhisattva (in Japanese *bosatsu*): a being of great spiritual attainment who is destined for Buddhahood, but who delays becoming a Buddha in order to help all others achieve this state.

bonsai: the art of dwarfing trees or plants by growing and training them in containers.

Children's Day: Festival held on May 5. Since ancient times, the day has been a festival for boys, corresponding to the Doll Festival for girls on March 3. In 1948, renamed Children's Day.

daimyō: landholding military lords in premodern Japan.

furoshiki: a square cloth used for wrapping and carrying objects.

futon: padded mattress and quilt which are pliable enough to be folded and stored out of sight during the day.

futonji: bridal bed quilt covers made of indigo-dyed cotton, which village artisans decorated with auspicious motifs and family crests.

haniwa: unglazed, cylindrical figures of people and animals that are the earliest examples of Japanese pottery. They were arranged in patterns, partially embedded in the earth, around the great mounded tombs built for the Japanese elite during the 4th to 7th centuries.

haori: a short kimono-style jacket worn over the kimono. The front is left open rather than overlapped and is tied with silk cords.

hibachi: an indoor brazier used to provide warmth, boil water for tea, or warm saké. It is made in a variety of sizes and materials, especially wood and ceramic, and is filled with sand and ash. Charcoal is arranged in the center under a trivet which supports a kettle.

ikat: see kasuri

Imari: see Arita ware

Karatsu ware: collective name for various ceramics produced south of the city of Karatsu, an ancient port in Hizen Province (now Saga Prefecture), Kyushu.

kasuri: a technique for fabric decoration in which warp and sometimes weft threads are tied and dyed before weaving. This selective dyeing, planned to produce a predetermined pattern, results in a hazy design called *kasuri* from the word "to blur." This resist dying technique is also called "ikat" from the Malay word "to tie" or "bind."

katazome: ancient technique for textile design. Rice paste is applied to fabric through a special paper stencil in order to resist dye in selected areas. Stencils are made of *kozo* (paper mulberry tree) and are strengthened by a coating of persimmon juice, so they can be cut with precision and used repeatedly. After the initial dyeing, the uncovered areas of the cloth are hand-painted.

kotatsu: wooden lattice table positioned over a heat source, often a *hibachi*, and covered with a quilt. Floor-seated people place their legs under the quilt for warmth.

Living National Treasure: Popular term for craftsmen and artists who have received the Japanese government's ultimate award for their mastery of a particular traditional skill. They are officially called "Bearers of Important Intangile Cultural Assets."

Ming: Chinese dynasty that ruled from 1368 to 1644 and was noted for artistic works produced during its reign.

ninja: secret agent or practitioner of ancient art of *ninjutsu* or subterfuge, a supposedly magical art for making oneself invisible by artifice or stratagem in order to evade detection.

obi: wide sash worn around the waist with a kimono.

Omote Senke: one of the three principal tea schools founded in the 17th century by the three great-grandsons of Tea Master Sen no Rikyu. The Omote Senke School catered to aristocracy. The other two schools, which also trace their lineage back 16 generations, are Ura Senke and Mushanokoji Senke.

origami: art of folding paper to form figures and objects.

prefecture: geographic territory empowered with administrating government within its region. The first prefectures were created in 1871 replacing feudal domaines, and now number 47.

saké: brewed, alcoholic beverage made from fermented rice.

samurai: warrior elite who ruled from the late 12th century to 1868.

sashiko: garments made of one or more layers of indigo-dyed hemp or cotton fabric and quilted in various patterns for the purpose of mending, reinforcement, warmth or decoration.

Satsuma ware: ceramic ware for the tea ceremony and general use made at kiln sites in Kagoshima Prefecture, formerly the Satsuma domaine, in southern Kyushu.

Shigaraki: stoneware produced by several villages in the Shigaraki valley in southern Shiga Prefecture. Can be identified by white specks and grains of feldspar and quartz that melt during firing and protrude from the surface.

soba: thin, buckwheat noodles served either in a soup or plain with a dipping sauce.

sumi: charcoal or soot-based, Chinese ink used for **sumi-e,** a Chinese style of painting which has been practiced by the Japanese since the 14th century. The medium offers a potentially infinite range of ink values.

sumo: form of wrestling with a 2,000-year history that rivals baseball in popularity in Japan.

tatami: a straw mat covered with woven rush, approximately 6' x 3', used as flooring material.

teaburi: small *hibachi* used for warming hands.

Tokoname ware: strong, reddish-

Index

brown ware made from the early 12th century to the first half of the 16th with some production continuing to the present. The kilns are distributed throughout the Chita Peninsula south of Nagoya.

Tokugawa Shogunate: the last and longest-lived of Japan's three warrior governments, 1603-1867.

tsutsugaki: literally "tube drawing," a resist-dyeing technique in which a design is drawn on fabric by squeezing rice paste through the tip of a cone-shaped tube. The freehand patterns made with the paste remain uncolored when dyes or pigments are applied to the cloth. The technique was used on a variety of utilitarian textiles and garments to celebrate auspicious occasions.

washi: hand-molded paper made principally from three kinds of trees: *kozo* (paper mulberry), *gampi* or *mitsumata* (which have no English translations).

yukata: informal, cotton, kimono-style robe worn in warm weather or for lounging.

Zen: meditation school of East Asian Buddhism.